THE BEST SWISS TRAIN RIDES

The Best Swiss Train Rides
35 unforgettable trips in the heart of Europe

Author: Diccon Bewes
Photography: See page 228 for photo credits
Cover design: Lucie Morat
Typesetting and layout: Fabian Lang
Editor: Angela Wade

ISBN: 978-3-03964-085-0
First edition: April 2025
Deposit copy in Switzerland: April 2025
Printed in the Czech Republic

Mittlere Strasse 4
4056 Basel
Switzerland

helvetiq.com

DICCON BEWES

THE BEST SWISS TRAIN RIDES

35 UNFORGETTABLE TRIPS IN THE HEART OF EUROPE

CONTENTS

Long-distance routes that cross over regions, e.g. the Gotthard Railway, only appear once in the book. Some train rides, such as the Glacier Express, can be done in sections; each stage is listed in the Index.

148

OVERVIEW MAP

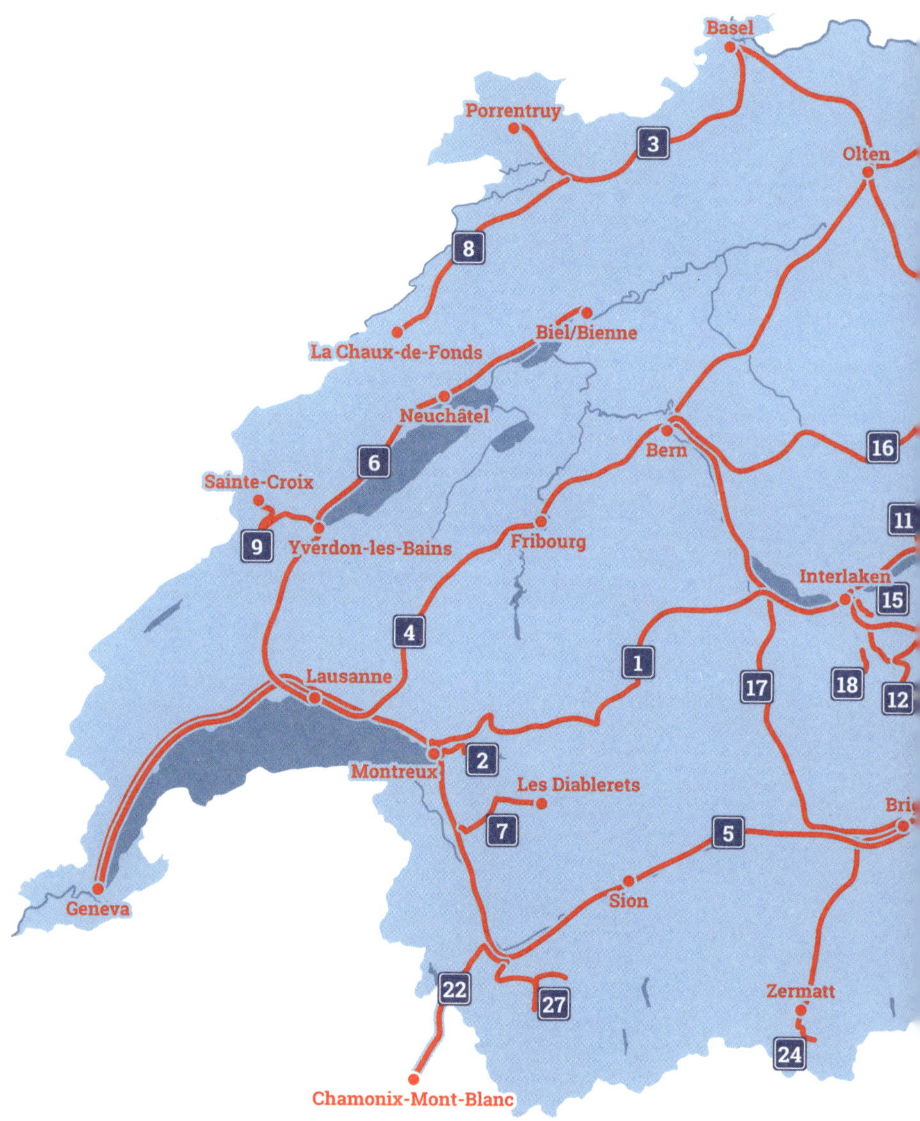

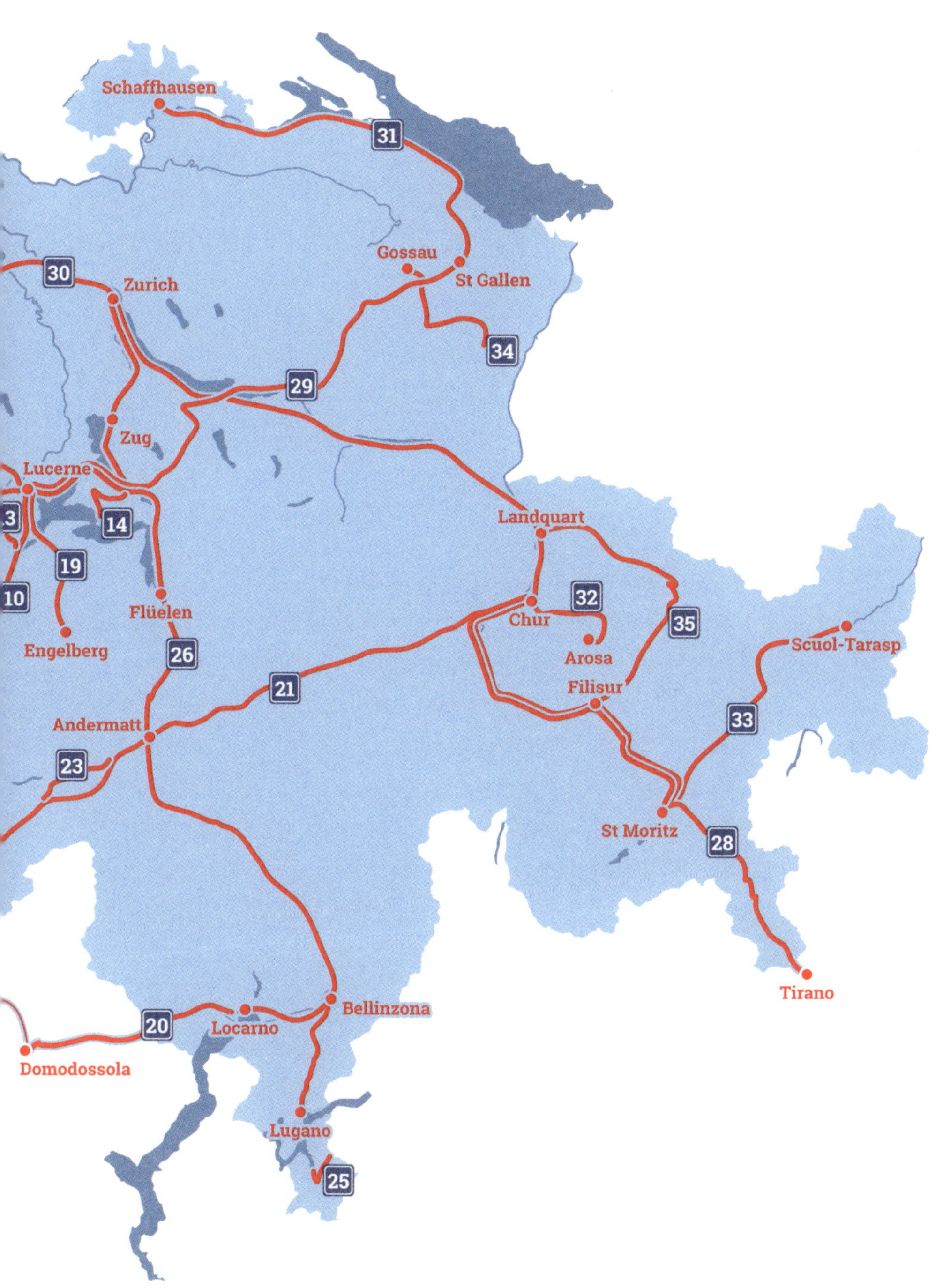

Schaffhausen
31
Gossau
St Gallen
30
Zurich
34
29
Zug
Lucerne
14
19
10
Engelberg
Flüelen
26
Landquart
32
Chur
35
Arosa
Filisur
Scuol-Tarasp
33
21
Andermatt
23
St Moritz
28
Tirano
Bellinzona
20
Locarno
Domodossola
Lugano
25

INTRODUCTION

Longest, highest, steepest – no, it's not the new slogan for the Olympics but some of the records that the Swiss rail network holds: the world's longest rail tunnel, the highest train station in Europe and the steepest railway in the world. Plus the Swiss come top of the global train travel stats when it comes to distance travelled per person each year. And I contribute to those stats: I love my annual travel pass, known as a GA or 'Generalabonnement' in German, and have seen the whole country through the window of a train.

The 35 trips in this book include all my favourite Swiss train rides. Of course, the big names are here, from the Glacier Express to the GoldenPass Line, as are the famous rack railways, such as Pilatus or Jungfraujoch. But this book also covers main line services and local narrow-gauge railways, many of which often get overlooked when talking about scenic rides. Every chapter has a description of the route with crucial details such as the journey time, altitude differences and where to sit in the train.

And every chapter includes the history of that route, which is often as captivating as the scenery, given that the trains had to go up, under or round the mountains. After the first Swiss line opened in August 1847, progress was initially slow but then the boom really began. For example, between 1890 and 1893, a quarter of the railways in this book were inaugurated – see the timeline at the end of the book for more details. Now let's explore Switzerland by train.

GOLDENPASS
EXPRESS

WESTERN SWITZERLAND

1 GOLDENPASS LINE

From lake to lake past mountains and chalets, this panoramic train is a ride to remember.

This trip between Interlaken and Montreux is as Swiss as Swiss can be. Not only does it pass through a landscape that's almost too cliché to be true, it also relies on advanced technology to make the whole journey. Your eyes can feast on a parade of cows on green hillsides, villages of dark wood chalets and the Alps crowning the skyline. And beneath your feet, the train does clever things you aren't even aware of.

Things get more complicated when it comes to choosing your train. Three different services run along the same route, all called the GoldenPass but with separate timetables and separate pages on the website. It can be confusing, especially when reserving a seat (recommended during busy periods). Only one – the GoldenPass Express – runs directly between Interlaken and Montreux; for the other two, you must change in Zweisimmen. The good news is the views are great whichever train you're on.

FAST FACTS

START
Interlaken

DISTANCE
115km

HEIGHT DIFFERENCE
874m

PASSES
GA & Swiss Travel Pass: free;
Half Fare card: 50% discount

END
Montreux

TIME NEEDED
3h 20min

WHERE TO SIT
On the right then left

NEARBY LINES
Rochers-de-Naye 2
Geneva–Brig 5
The Lötschberger 17

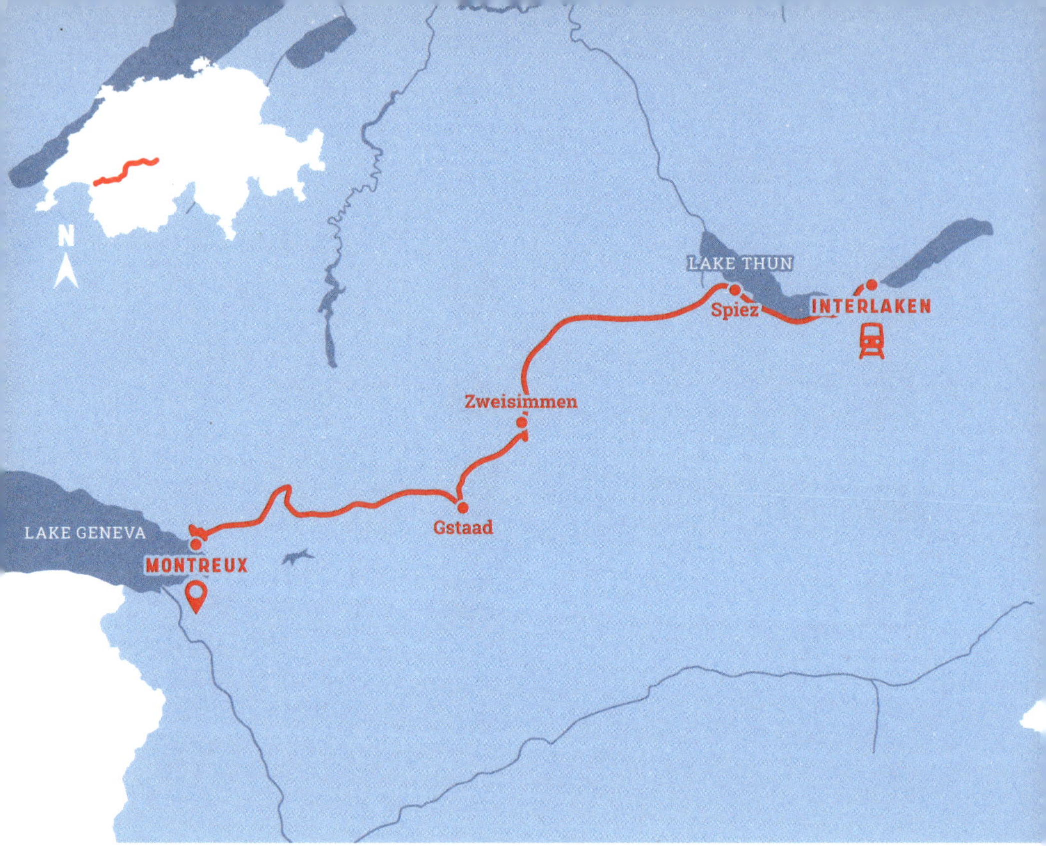
N
LAKE THUN
Spiez
INTERLAKEN
Zweisimmen
Gstaad
LAKE GENEVA
MONTREUX

1300 m
1200 m
1100 m
1000 m
900 m
800 m
700 m
600 m
500 m
400 m
INTERLAKEN
Spiez
Zweisimmen
Gstaad
MONTREUX

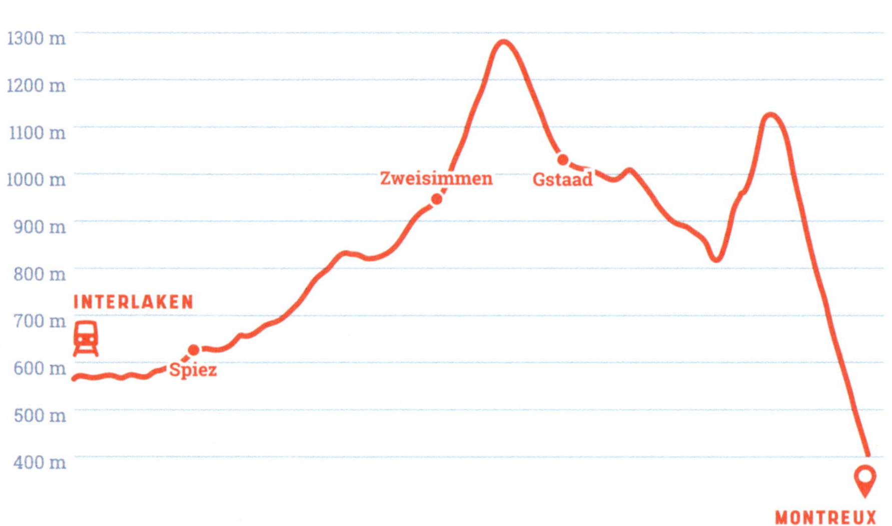

THE ROUTE

Sit on the right in Interlaken, as you skim along the edge of Lake Thun, for picture-perfect photos of the majestic scenery to Spiez. The line curls round into the Simmental, with classic valley views of wooden chalets scattered on steep hillsides with rocky escarpments above. And of course, the trademark brown-and-white Simmental breed of cows.

At Zweisimmen the gauges change (and maybe also where you change trains) but the scenery remains as bucolic. This isn't a fast train, so you have time to enjoy gently meandering through the hills, with the skyline getting ever more mountainous as the line climbs to its highest point (1269m) and then descends to the swish resort village of Gstaad. From here on, switch to the left for the best views, especially once you cross the (invisible) language border.

Approaching Chateau d'Oex, look left for the perfect view of three jagged peaks towering over wooded hills and green pastures. After that, the route gets narrower, with sheer cliff faces and steep drops on the left, until there's the first glimpse of Lake Geneva, which gets larger the lower the line goes. Finally, the train dramatically switchbacks left-right-left-right to descend through the vineyards to Montreux – with lake views all the way.

THE HISTORY

A 1922 poster with views of Lake Geneva along the GoldenPass Line.

Two lines built by two companies in two directions with two gauges: so for decades a change of trains was necessary in Zweisimmen, at least until modern technology overcame that hurdle. At the Lake Geneva end, it began with the founding of the Montreux Oberland Bernois Railway in 1899. Construction began soon after, using a metre gauge to tackle the altitude difference, with the line to Zweisimmen opening in July 1905. It was the first railway in Switzerland to be completely electric – and later (in 1976) the first to introduce a panorama car.

At Lake Thun, the main railway from Spiez to Interlaken was in operation from 1893, and a branch line up the Simmental followed soon after; the final stretch to Zweisimmen opened in October 1902. But, like the main line, it was built with a standard gauge (the distance between the rails) of 1435mm. Calling it the GoldenPass Line came in 1916, even with the obligatory change of trains, but plans for a third rail failed to gain traction. Eventually in 2008 it was decided to change the trains, not the tracks, using a variable gauge bogie to bridge the 435mm gap. There was also the matter of the two railways having different platform heights and different voltages but it worked: on 11 December 2022 the Express was inaugurated.

TRIP TIPS

Two GoldenPass trains run between Zweisimmen and Montreux. The Panoramic is the regular, frequent service, usually with both panoramic carriages (the ones with glass roof panels) as well as standard ones. I prefer the latter, as they have windows that open: great for fresh air and glass-free photos.

Or there's the delightful Belle Epoque service with its elegant nostalgic carriages, although that only operates twice a day. For either train, you first need to reach Zweisimmen (or carry on from there if going in the opposite direction): take a normal BLS train from Spiez to connect with the GoldenPass trains. It's an easy change just across the platform.

The GoldenPass Express has an extra special class called Prestige. You need a first-class ticket (plus the mandatory seat reservation fee) to enjoy more room and rotating seats that are raised higher than usual to give you better views. The Express runs four times a day and is the only one that travels the whole route.

2 ROCHERS-DE-NAYE

A short steep rack railway that goes high above Montreux for stunning views of Lake Geneva and the Alps.

Standing on the lakeshore in Montreux and looking up to the peaks towering above the town, it's almost impossible to believe that in under an hour, you could be up there looking down. But thanks to the 19th-century craze for building mountain trains purely for tourists, it's an easy trip to Rochers-de-Naye, almost 1600m above Lake Geneva. The wonderful views of Western Europe's largest lake and most of the Alps always make me whisper a word of thanks to those long-gone engineers.

The railway ends at 1973m, just short of the summit, which clocks in at 2042m. The station faces east, with views from the restaurant terrace over the hills, so you have to walk to get panorama shots that include the lake. A flat pedestrian tunnel ends at the dramatic viewpoint looking west across Lake Geneva and down to Montreux. Or it's a hearty hike up to the summit for a 360° panorama of the whole region and a skyline packed with peaks.

FAST FACTS

START
Montreux

END
Rochers-de-Naye

DISTANCE
7.6km

TIME NEEDED
48min

HEIGHT DIFFERENCE
1578m

WHERE TO SIT
On the left

PASSES
GA: free; Swiss Travel Pass: free halfway then 50%; Half Fare card: 50% discount

NEARBY LINES
GoldenPass Line 1
Geneva–Brig 5
Mont-Blanc Express 22

304
MONTREUX-GLION
ROCHERS DE NAYE

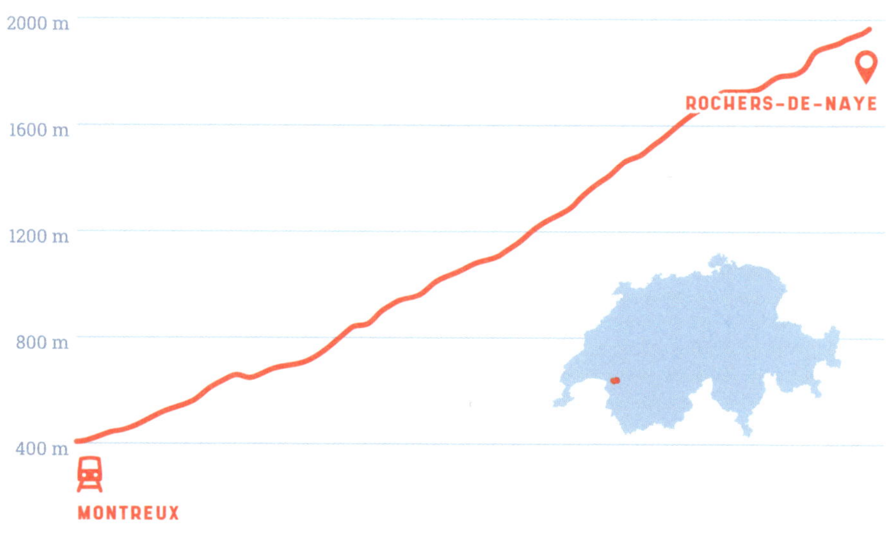
2000 m
1600 m
1200 m
800 m
400 m
ROCHERS-DE-NAYE
MONTREUX

THE ROUTE

There's nothing modern about the nostalgic carriages still used on this line: as the train jiggles its way out of Montreux station, it's like you're travelling back in time. After the first tunnel, you emerge behind the houses and climb steadily upwards, with glimpses of the lake on the right. Another long, curling tunnel and the lake is now on the left – on balance, the best side to sit.

The station at Glion has a backdrop of the lake and mountains in all their glory: no wonder the funicular came up here long before the train. The line goes steeper and steeper stopping at stations on vertiginous inclines, and with views alternating between left and right. Thickly-wooded slopes lead up to pyramidal rocks with exposed folding strata and sheer drop-offs.

Another tunnel then you reach Buvette de Jaman, a popular stop for hikers wanting to tackle the Dent de Jaman, a jagged tooth of a mountain above the station. As you go uphill, look for the sign marking the watershed between the Rhine and the Rhone rivers. With sharp rocky ridges to the left and a last view of the lake on the right, you enter a final tunnel and come out at the top of the line.

THE HISTORY

Poster from 1900, when the railway still started in Glion.

In the summer of 1892, trains reached Rochers-de-Naye for the first time, unloading hundreds of happy tourists eager to enjoy the views. But those tourists had not boarded the train in Montreux as we do today. Back then the rack railway built by the Glion Rochers-de-Naye Railway only started in Glion, high above Montreux. It was reached by a funicular from Territet, down by the lake, which had opened in 1883 as the world's steepest funicular; it's still in operation today, though it's no longer necessary to use it to start your trip.

The direct connection to Glion was achieved in April 1909 when the rack railway finally started in Montreux itself. Oddly, the new section was electric from the beginning but the old section was steam-powered until 1938 so that carriages had to be handed over from electric to steam locomotives at Glion. This new section was built by the Montreux-Glion Railway, which had no platform space in Montreux so it bought a hotel next to the station, demolished it and built its own platform. The two separate train companies merged in 1986 and then became part of Montreux-Vevey-Riviera Transport, along with the Territet-Glion funicular.

TRIP TIPS

Unusually for a mountain train trip, the whole ride is included in the GA travel pass so you can just hop on board. For Swiss Travel Pass holders, it's only free as far as Haut-de-Caux (roughly halfway) – to go beyond there, you must buy a ticket, although you get a 50% discount. Half Fare cards are valid for the whole journey.

As great as they are, the views aren't the only reason to come to Rochers-de-Naye. There are also resident marmots, which really are as cute as they appear, and in summer months it's worth visiting the Alpine garden with over 1000 species of plants. And there are various hikes, of course.

On the return journey, you could get off at Glion and switch to one of the oldest public funiculars in Switzerland for the six-minute ride down to Territet. From there, it's a gentle walk alongside the water's edge back to Montreux.

3 BASEL ↔ PORRENTRUY

A local line spanning both town and country, winding through limestone gorges south of the French border.

This route might start in Switzerland's third-largest city but it quickly moves into the dramatic gorge of the River Birs and on through the hilly landscapes of Canton Jura. On a map it cuts a flat-bottomed U shape, mirroring the course of the French border to the north, to reach Porrentruy. Once the residence of the prince-bishops of Basel, this oft-overlooked town has a handsome medieval centre and impressive castle.

If the station at Porrentruy seems too grand for such a small town, it's because this was once the main railway line from France to Switzerland. Thanks to different borders and geopolitical interests, it was a busy international route for freight and passengers until the First World War. It's still international today, with a new cross-border connection, but it's much quieter than in its heyday: perfect for gentle exploring.

FAST FACTS

START
Basel

END
Porrentruy

DISTANCE
67km

TIME NEEDED
1h 13min

HEIGHT DIFFERENCE
228m

WHERE TO SIT
Either side

PASSES
GA & Swiss Travel Pass: free;
Half Fare card: 50% discount

NEARBY LINES
Lausanne–Biel/Bienne 6
Jura Railways 8
Gotthard Railway 26

THE ROUTE

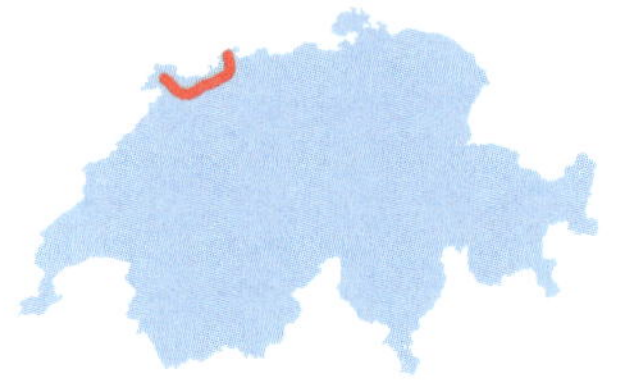

Starting in Basel, it's perhaps no surprise that the first part of this trip is high-rises then suburban houses. But the hills soon appear and, all at once, you're in the steep-sided valley of the River Birs, with towering cliffs on the right. It feels beautifully untamed after all the urban sprawl.

The single-track railway threads its way through the gorge, crossing and re-crossing the river, sometimes passing a field of wheat but mainly surrounded by rock and wood. Look up on the cliff tops for the ruined castle at Pfeffingen and the pretty Chappelle du Vorbourg outside Delémont.

After the Jura capital, the train switches to another winding river, the Doubs, cutting across its course with tunnels and bridges, including the majestic 12-arch Combe Maran viaduct – look left for a perfect view of the walled village of St-Ursanne (pictured below). Our last stop is Porrentruy, although the line carries on to Delle in France.

THE HISTORY

Porrentruy station in the 1930s, after its heyday as the main route to France.

Switzerland's first railway station opened in 1844 in Basel, as the terminus of a French railway from Strasbourg. But losing the Franco-Prussian War in 1871 meant that France also lost Alsace-Lorraine and access to their station in Basel. A new route from France was built in stages through the Jura mountains, starting from the border town of Delle to Porrentruy in 1872. The line from Basel to Delémont opened three years later, with the final connection following in March 1877.

Porrentruy became the fourth largest freight station in Switzerland, with a vast customs depot, but it was also busy with passenger traffic: in the summer of 1914, 11 daily express trains passed through, including the Engadin Express, a direct train from Calais to Chur. Once France regained Alsace-Lorraine, this line became less important and cross-border trains were eventually discontinued in the 1990s. They were resurrected in 2018, which then enabled a connection to the TGV line at Meroux.

4 BERN ↔ GENEVA

Main line Intercity route that would probably be classed as a scenic train ride in most other countries.

It's a classic moment of railway drama: as the train emerges from a tunnel about halfway from Bern to Geneva, a panoramic view suddenly opens up. Sunlight-dappled water stretches off into the distance with the jagged peaks of the French mountains across the lake. At least that's what you see if you sit on the left-hand side; sit on the right and all you see is rocks and grass. The funny thing is that this celebrated view of Lake Geneva almost didn't happen.

The main Intercity route runs right across the country from Lake Constance in the east to Geneva in the west. It's one of the busiest lines in Switzerland and this is its western section, linking the capital with the two largest cities in Romandie. But it was built piecemeal at different times by different companies. Back before SBB, railway lines were based on concessions granted by the cantons, and this route needed an intervention in Federal Parliament to resolve a fierce cantonal dispute.

FAST FACTS

START
Bern

DISTANCE
129km

HEIGHT DIFFERENCE
367m

PASSES
GA & Swiss Travel Pass: free;
Half Fare card: 50% discount

END
Geneva

TIME NEEDED
1h 51min

WHERE TO SIT
On the left towards Geneva

NEARBY LINES
Lausanne–Biel/Bienne 6
Bern–Lucerne 16
The Lötschberger 17

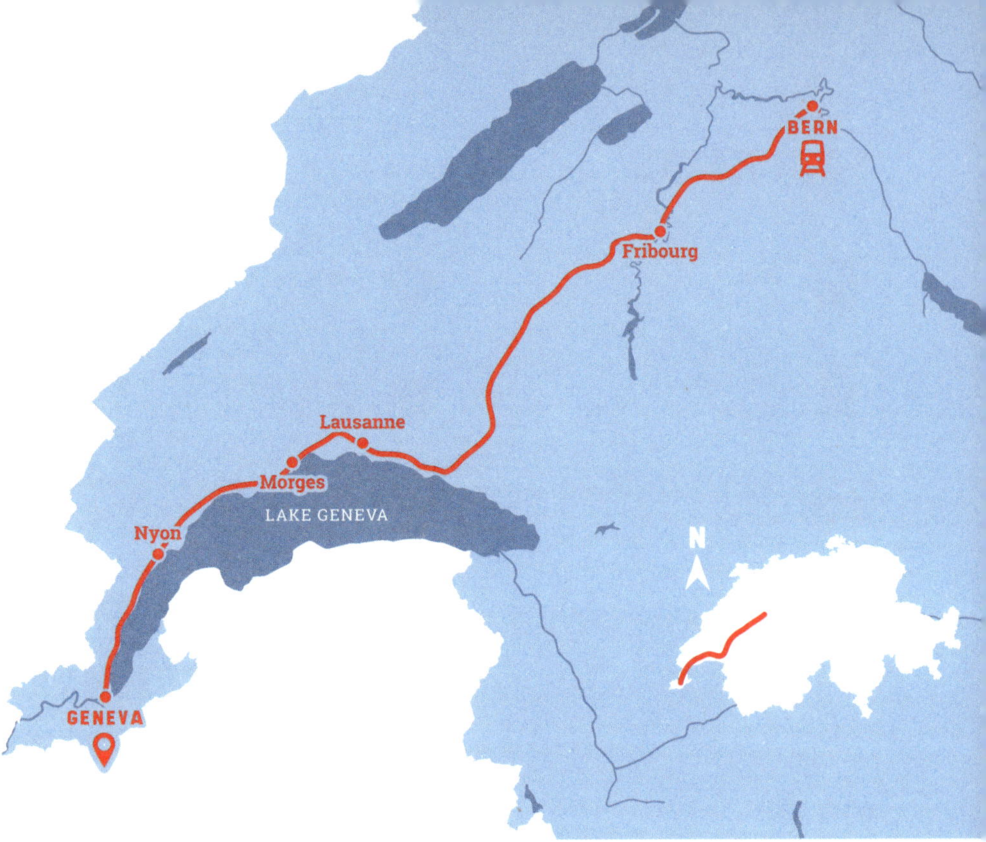

BERN
Fribourg
Lausanne
Morges
LAKE GENEVA
Nyon
GENEVA
N

700 m
600 m
500 m
400 m
Fribourg
BERN
Lausanne
Nyon
Morges
GENEVA

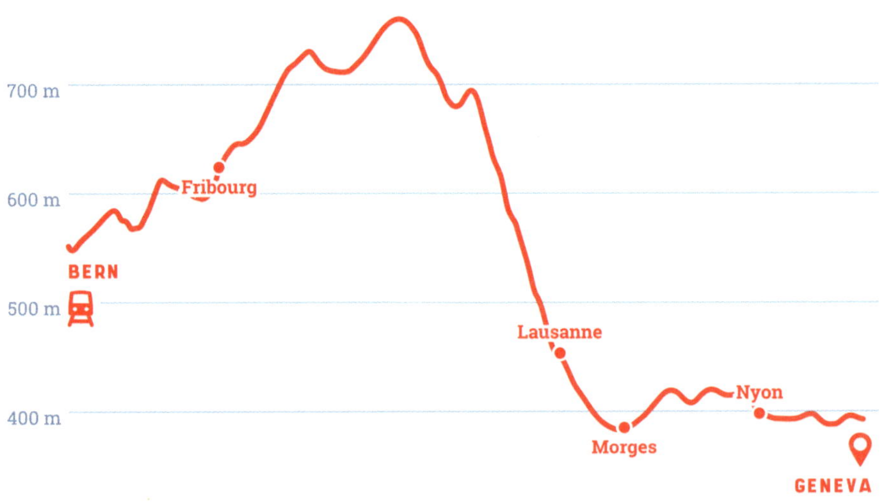

THE ROUTE

Once past the suburbs of Bern, it's all green hills and cow-dotted pastures, with an occasional rugged mountain on the left-hand side. Just before Fribourg, you cross both the language border from German to French and the River Saane/Sarine via one of the largest rail bridges in Switzerland, the Grandfey Viaduct (pictured below).

The wow moment comes after Palézieux as you emerge from the Grandvaux tunnel to see Lake Geneva for the first time. Even on a murky grey day, it's still grand, with vineyards clinging to the steep hills and the mountains as a backdrop. Doing this trip in reverse from Geneva to Bern brings the same views, except for this famous shot of the lake. There's no wow moment because you're leaving the lake behind.

The line descends to Lausanne then follows the long arc of Lake Geneva, never quite by the water but never far from it, so you see glimpses of it on the left-hand side now and then. On an Intercity train, there are no stops until Geneva, making it a fast, pleasant ride of 35 minutes to Cornavin station. This current incarnation opened in 1931, after the original was destroyed by fire.

THE HISTORY

It's hard to imagine that a railway line could engineer a cantonal conflict but this one did. By 1858 the line from Geneva to Lausanne was complete but there was no connection to Bern, thanks to a disagreement between the cantons of Fribourg and Vaud. The original route selected, via Yverdon and Murten, was flatter but bypassed the city of Fribourg. Oddly enough, that wasn't popular in Fribourg so it proposed a competing route via Oron that was shorter but through more difficult terrain.

Each route involved building through the opposing canton's territory, which neither canton would permit. Both applied to Federal Parliament for compulsory concessions to force the other side into submission. Parliament finally chose the shorter Oron route and the concession was granted to the Lausanne-Fribourg-Bern Railway (LFB). The line opened in September 1862, completing the link between Geneva and German-speaking Switzerland. LFB eventually morphed into Jura-Simplon Railways, the largest train company in Switzerland, before the creation of the SBB, and builders of the Simplon Tunnel to Italy.

Swiss Federal Railways poster from 1926 advertising the delights of Geneva.

TRIP TIPS

Instead of whizzing straight to Geneva, why not stop off along the way? Twenty minutes from Bern is Fribourg, capital of the eponymous canton and the reason this line takes this particular route. The bilingual city (it's Freiburg in German) is home to an elegant cathedral and medieval town walls.

Lausanne has one of the most imposing stations in Switzerland – it's worth getting off the train just to admire the handsome structure that opened in 1916. Take a peek in the old station buffet to see how grand train journeys once were. You could also hop on to Switzerland's only metro to glide downhill to lakeside Ouchy, or give your calves a workout and walk up to the hilltop cathedral.

Take the hourly InterRegio train instead of the Intercity and you benefit from extra stops between the main cities. Morges and Nyon both sit on the northern shore of Lake Geneva: both have impressive castles and both are perfect for a spot of lunch or a wander around the old town.

5 GENEVA ↔ BRIG

Classic lake-and-mountains train ride along the Rhone Valley from Lake Geneva into the heart of the Valais Alps.

As the train glides effortlessly through the terraced vineyards, it gets closer and closer to the water until it feels like the wheels might actually get wet. The railway from Geneva eastwards runs right beside Lac Léman (as the great lake is known in French) then up along the flattish Rhone Valley. That means it has no great altitude changes, but it makes up for that with close-up views of the lake and wide-angle ones of the surrounding peaks.

This busy line along the lakeshore doesn't always have multiple tracks (much to the annoyance of residents and visitors alike) but it is a multi-use railway. Alongside the regional and local trains are also the fast Eurocity connections to Milan. All of them follow the same route, and have the same views, but the slower the train, the more chances you have to get off and explore the Lavaux wineries or historic towns.

FAST FACTS

START
Geneva

END
Brig

DISTANCE
206km

TIME NEEDED
2h 27min

HEIGHT DIFFERENCE
303m

WHERE TO SIT
On the right towards Brig

PASSES
GA & Swiss Travel Pass: free;
Half Fare card: 50% discount

NEARBY LINES
GoldenPass Line 1
Glacier Express 21
Mont-Blanc Express 22

Lausanne
LAKE GENEVA
GENEVA
Martigny
Sion
BRIG
N
BRIG
600 m
500 m
400 m
GENEVA
Lausanne
Martigny
Sion

THE ROUTE

The first section from Geneva isn't anything to write home about: pleasant but with only fleeting glimpses of the lake and handsome towns like Nyon. Then from Lausanne onwards, there's plenty going on outside the window, starting with the marshalled rows of vines that run right up to the tracks. Come in autumn and the train glides through a sea of golden leaves against a bright blue backdrop.

After Cully the lake is so close you can almost reach out and touch it (if only the windows could be opened). Sandwiched between wine and water, this ride through the Lavaux is Swiss perfection, all the way to genteel Montreux. Here the vines are replaced by villas – and look out for the mighty medieval Chillon Castle on the right.

Leaving the lake behind, the train heads upstream along the Rhone, with the valley becoming quite narrow in places, such as around the 90° bend at Martigny. Then it's on through acres of orchards and past the twin peaks of Sion (sit on the left here for the best view of the castles). As the mountains get bigger and steeper, and the Rhone gets ever milkier, the train arrives in Brig.

THE HISTORY

Thanks to the success of Swiss Federal Railways, it can be hard to grasp the fairly chaotic beginnings of the train system in Switzerland. This line is a good example of how things used to be. Even though on a map it looks like a simple proposition to build a railway along the Rhone Valley, it was constructed piecemeal by private companies with different priorities in various cantons. The first part, built by the Compagnie de l'Ouest Suisse between Renens and Morges, opened on 1 July 1855, making it one of the oldest train lines in Switzerland.

Sections were gradually added so that Geneva was linked to Lausanne, though until 1861 boats had to be used to reach the east end of Lake Geneva. In the Rhone Valley itself, the Ligne d'Italie built its line from the lake to Sion, with plans to extend it along the southern lakeshore, at least until Savoy was annexed by France in 1860. Ligne d'Italie went bankrupt but its successor, Compagnie du Simplon, completed the railway to Brig on 1 June 1878. All the companies eventually merged into the Jura-Simplon Railways, which extended the line to Italy via the Simplon Tunnel.

A 1895 Jura-Simplon Railways poster from French artist F. Hugo d'Alési.

TRIP TIPS

If you want to hop off at smaller stations and walk among the vineyards, switch to a local train between Lausanne and Montreux, and stroll along the lakeshore, maybe even indulging in some wine-tasting as you go. You could also take a very relaxing boat ride on this section of Lake Geneva.

One highlight of this route is the many castles along the way, most of which can be visited. The scene-stealer is Chillon, possibly the finest in Switzerland, but I also like the ones at Nyon, Morges, Aigle and Sion (pictured below). There's also the impressive Stockalper Castle in Brig, with its three towers topped by onion domes.

Of course, the train doesn't reach a dead-end in Brig. The main line carries on into Italy via the Simplon Tunnel, which opened in 1906 as the fastest way south to Milan. Or you can take the high route to follow the Rhone upstream before descending into the Rhine Valley, a line also known as the Glacier Express.

6 LAUSANNE ↔ BIEL/BIENNE

A relaxed Intercity route in the heart of French-speaking Switzerland, alongside lakes and the Jura foothills.

Sandwiched between mountains and lakes, this trip is one of the flattest in Switzerland, with very little difference in altitude. And that's the reason it was among the first railways to be built back in the 1850s, when lines were planned along the routes of least resistance. Today, it provides a scenic connection for the towns and cities of Suisse Romande, with waterside views and Alpine skylines.

This forms a central part of the western route between Geneva and Zurich, offering an Intercity alternative to the busier main line via Bern – particularly important when either line has a problem. At Ligerz on Lake Biel, the last single-track section of the whole railway has long been a bottleneck, with no way round. A new 2km-long double-track tunnel is being built to replace this pinch-point and will open in 2029.

FAST FACTS

START
Lausanne

DISTANCE
105km

HEIGHT DIFFERENCE
85m

PASSES
GA & Swiss Travel Pass: free;
Half Fare card: 50% discount

END
Biel/Bienne

TIME NEEDED
1h 8min

WHERE TO SIT
On the right towards Biel/Bienne

NEARBY LINES
Bern–Geneva 4
Geneva–Brig 5
Yverdon–Sainte-Croix 9

THE ROUTE

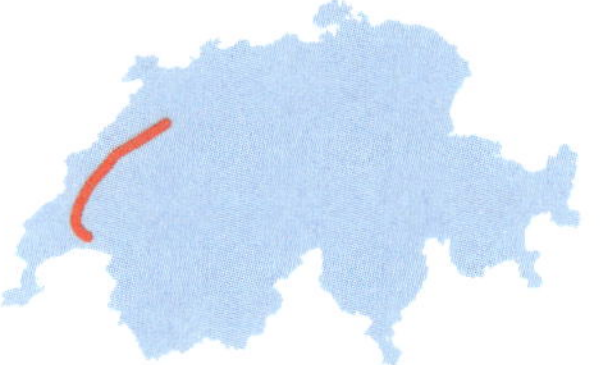

It takes a while to leave the last of Lausanne's suburbs behind but eventually the train slides past Bussigny and heads north through the rolling hills and (in summer) fields of sunflowers. The first main stop is Yverdon-les-Bains, with just the briefest glimpse of the handsome castle.

The line then mostly hugs the shore of Lake Neuchâtel, the largest lake entirely within Switzerland. Often you're right beside the water, with the chain of Alps across the lake on the eastern horizon so sit on the right all the way. Coming in to Neuchâtel, there's a picture-perfect view of the castle and Collegiate church.

A short hop across flat farmland and the train reaches its second lake, that of Biel, with glittering water on the right and stacked vineyards on the left. The lakeshore is an appealing hotchpotch of houses, vines, allotments and the occasional lido, all with views across to the hills. One long tunnel takes you into bilingual Biel/Bienne.

THE HISTORY

On 7 May 1855 the third railway line in Switzerland opened, adding to those already in operation on the Zurich-Baden and Basel-Liestal routes. This latest line ran from Yverdon-les-Bains to Bussigny, just northwest of Lausanne, and two months later was quickly extended to Renens. The railway was built by the Compagnie de l'Ouest Suisse, which planned to construct a line all the way to Bern via Murten. Those plans were thwarted by a rival route, via Fribourg, being built.

Instead, the extension followed a more northerly course, along the shores of Lakes Neuchâtel and Biel, making the most of the flat landscape. By 1859 the railway had reached the open land between the two lakes and a year later, on 3 December 1860, it arrived in Biel/Bienne. That town already had a station, thanks to the Swiss Central Railway, which had built its own line from Solothurn westwards in 1857. Today, this route remains a vital east-west connection across Switzerland.

Jura-Simplon Railways poster from 1895 painted by French artist F. Hugo d'Alési.

7 AIGLE ↔ LES DIABLERETS

A short but scenic trip from the broad plain of the River Rhone up into the heart of the Vaud Alps.

Start with a castle surrounded by vines, add a vertiginous V of a valley, throw in thousands of trees and end with a view of imposing mountains. If that sounds like the perfect recipe for a great train ride, then the result is this little railway in Canton Vaud. It may be short but it's sweet and steep (though isn't a rack railway) and runs all year round.

This was a railway that was originally meant to go over the Col du Pillon and connect with the Montreux Oberland Bernois Railway. What an amazing trip that would have been! Sadly, this line never made it past Les Diablerets, though the trip up there is worth it anyway. But then you must disembark in the shadow of the many lofty peaks and catch a bus to finish the beautiful journey to Glacier 3000 or Gstaad by road.

FAST FACTS

START
Aigle

DISTANCE
23km

HEIGHT DIFFERENCE
751m

PASSES
GA & Swiss Travel Pass: free;
Half Fare card: 50% discount

END
Les Diablerets

TIME NEEDED
50min

WHERE TO SIT
On the left

NEARBY LINES
GoldenPass Line 1
Rochers-de-Naye 2
Geneva–Brig 5

THE ROUTE

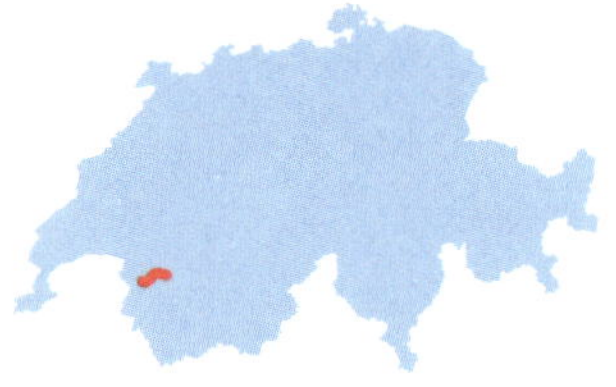

This is a train that thinks it's a tram, at least at first as it rumbles through the streets of Aigle, stopping in the Place du Marché. But then it's off into the countryside, winding past regimented vineyards with Aigle's grand medieval castle on the right.

The climb begins with wide S-bends through the vines and woods, with the best views on the left: first of the Rhone Valley, then the deep chasm of the Grande Eau. The railway hugs the right-hand slope, helped by tall viaducts and loop tunnels, while across on the left of the huge V is Leysin, with the main road clinging to the rock.

At Le Sépey, the train pulls in, the driver switches ends and the train pulls out, briefly back along the same line before heading upwards. An occasional farmhouse or isolated wooden station are the only breaks in the wild wooded landscape until the train reaches Les Diablerets and its impressive mountains.

THE HISTORY

Aigle station in 1946 when it was a little less busy than today.

Once the main line along the Rhone Valley had reached Aigle in 1857, it was only a matter of time before local railways started curling up into the mountains – although this one took a while to get going. The Aigle Sépey Diablerets Railway was founded in 1911, with a concession for a metre-gauge railway that was planned to go all the way to Gstaad.

The first section from Aigle to Le Sépey opened in December 1913, and the extension to Les Diablerets a few months later on 7 July 1914. Both sections were electric from the start. The line never progressed beyond Les Diablerets and the little railway was threatened with closure, especially after a disastrous fire in June 1940 destroyed the Aigle depot plus three trains and four carriages. But it was saved and in 1999 became part of TPC, or Transports Publics de Chablais.

8 JURA RAILWAYS

Slow travel at its best through the Jura hills with one of Switzerland's smallest train companies.

There's nothing fast about train travel here. It's only 51km from La Chaux-de-Fonds to Glovelier but the trip takes a leisurely 76 minutes as the metre-gauge railway meanders through the undulating countryside. This is a world away from busy mountain trains and crowded Intercity routes, so take the time to slow down and enjoy travelling through this relatively remote region of forests and farms.

Jura Railways is a small train company, operating a short Y-shaped network going northeast from La Chaux-de-Fonds, with the junction at Le Noirmont. There's a direct hourly service along the northern arm of the Y to Glovelier, where you can connect to SBB trains to Delémont. Reaching Tavannes (and so the SBB line to Moutier) at the end of the southern arm requires a change of trains. If you don't have time for the whole Y route, take the main arm to Glovelier, as described in this chapter.

FAST FACTS

START
La Chaux-de-Fonds

END
Glovelier

DISTANCE
51km

TIME NEEDED
1h 16min

HEIGHT DIFFERENCE
567m

WHERE TO SIT
On the left then right

PASSES
GA & Swiss Travel Pass: free; Half Fare card: 50% discount

NEARBY LINES
Basel–Porrentruy 3
Lausanne–Biel/Bienne 6
Yverdon–Sainte-Croix 9

THE ROUTE

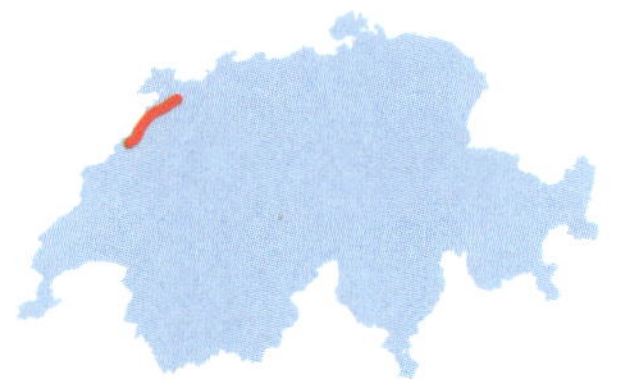

This Jura Railways line actually starts over the cantonal border in La Chaux-de-Fonds, famous for its watches. Just as well the little red train leaves on time, though at first it's more tram than train as it trundles through the streets. But the pine forests and green fields soon appear, with better views on the left.

Stops come every few minutes but most are 'Arrêt sur demande'; though there's little demand for some of the tiny stations that are merely a hut beside a meadow of cows. On past the junction at Le Noirmont, with connecting trains to Tavannes, and the horse town of Saignelégier, then the slow descent begins.

Views switch to the right, with a steep gorge of dense woods and limestone crags. Then, in the middle of nowhere, the train stops, the driver switches ends and the journey continues in the opposite direction, all to cope with the change in altitude. Much of the route lies at around 1000m but the terminus at Glovelier is half that.

THE HISTORY

The station at Le Noirmont in 1953, where the two branch lines meet.

Railways came to this region a bit later than the rest of the country. While the main line from Delémont to the French border was completed in 1877, there was no sign of a local line from Glovelier. That was partly down to topography but also to the fragmented nature of railway construction at that time. What is now Jura Railways started as four separate companies, which finally merged into one in 1944.

The oldest section of this railway is that between Tavannes and Tramelan, which opened in 1884 but 30 years later was extended to Le Noirmont.

Then followed the line between La Chaux-de-Fonds and Saignelégier in 1892, and 12 years later the onward line to Glovelier, where it could connect to the main line. Interestingly, that Saignelégier-Glovelier railway was built to a standard gauge of 1435mm, even though the others were metre gauge. In 1952, it too became a metre-gauge line.

9 YVERDON-LES-BAINS ↔ SAINTE-CROIX

Hit the heights of the Jura mountains with this lovely ride through the woods to reveal a grandstand view of the Alps.

In a country famous for its railways, there are many well-known trains that take you up or under the mountains; trains that attract thousands of guests each year. But there are also local lines tucked away in half-hidden corners that rarely make the headlines and are possibly not even known outside the region they serve. These are exactly the train trips I like to find, like the one up to Sainte-Croix.

The spa town of Yverdon-les-Bains sits at the southern end of Lake Neuchatel, separated from nearby France by the Jura mountains. Perched up in those mountains is Sainte-Croix, a village renowned for its mechanical music boxes. Perhaps that's why every stop is announced with a string of notes from a harp. And that's not the only relaxing thing about this gentle train ride; as it winds its way uphill, the views get better the higher you climb.

FAST FACTS

START
Yverdon-les-Bains

END
Sainte-Croix

DISTANCE
24km

TIME NEEDED
35min

HEIGHT DIFFERENCE
631m

WHERE TO SIT
On the right going uphill

PASSES
GA & Swiss Travel Pass: free;
Half Fare card: 50% discount

NEARBY LINES
Bern–Geneva 4
Lausanne–Biel/Bienne 6
Jura Railways 8

THE ROUTE

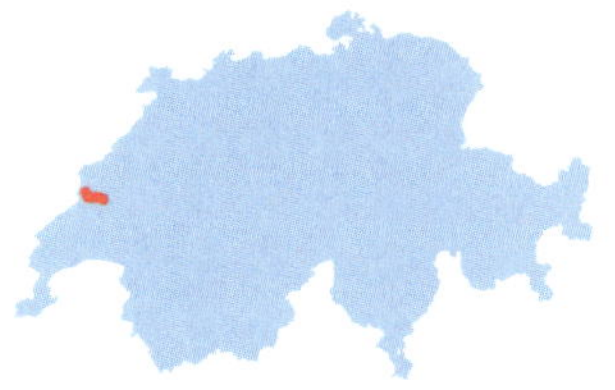

Not far from the turreted castle is Yverdon station, and not far from the main platforms are two narrow-gauge tracks off to the side. As the train trundles out, it feels like you're in an overgrown bus, especially as almost every stop is on request.

Soon you're heading for the hills, sandwiched between woodland and farmland, taking a sinuous course on the single-track line. Sit on the left at first, for views across the rolling hills to a skyline punctuated with peaks. After Six-Fontaines, switch to the right for the photo moment.

At first it's all trees, and then there it is: a panorama worthy of the name, from Lake Neuchatel to Mont Blanc, with all the Alps in between. A final flourish of harp music announces your arrival in Sainte-Croix, tucked away at the head of the Gorges de Covatannaz. For more of that widescreen Alps view, it's a short bus ride to Les Rasses for a drink on the terrace of the Grand Hotel.

THE HISTORY

Sainte-Croix station in 1921 when the railway still used steam engines.

Behind a simple fact – this line opened on 27 November 1893 – is a story that's unusual, if not unique. The railway to Sainte-Croix was planned and financed by one man, William Barbey, a botanist and politician from Canton Geneva. He had one main condition for 'his' railway: that trains could not run on Sundays (he was also against cars being used on Sundays). His religious ban on Sunday services lasted until shortly after his death in 1914.

At first, the metre-gauge line used steam engines but the outdated locomotives and a wartime shortage of coal made it essential to convert to electricity in 1945. One sad note in this line's history: on Saturday 14 February 1976 two trains crashed head on – seven people died and 43 were injured. The Yverdon–Sainte-Croix railway company merged in 2001 with other local transport providers to form TRAVYS, which now operates the line.

CENTRAL SWITZERLAND

10 LUZERN–INTERLAKEN EXPRESS

One of the premier lakes-and-mountains scenic train rides running right through the green heart of Switzerland.

Open a rail map of Switzerland and it's not too surprising to see a train line running between Lake Lucerne and the Bernese Oberland. They aren't very far apart as the crow flies and it's logical to link these two much-visited regions with a direct service. But look closer at the topography and you'll notice one relatively big hurdle to such a route: the Brünig Pass, the best way through the mountains but at 1008m high still a challenge.

Going up through that narrow pass is the high point of this bucolic train trip but not the only highlight. While it may not have the stunning drama of some other mountain lines, and a rather prosaic name, the Luzern–Interlaken Express has a gently bewitching appeal. As you roll through green fields, past glittering lakes and beneath craggy mountains, you'll slowly fall under its spell. It's hard to think of a more satisfyingly Swiss train ride.

FAST FACTS

START
Lucerne

DISTANCE
74km

HEIGHT DIFFERENCE
566m

PASSES
GA & Swiss Travel Pass: free;
Half Fare card: 50% discount

END
Interlaken

TIME NEEDED
1h 49min

WHERE TO SIT
On the right towards Interlaken

NEARBY LINES
Brienzer Rothorn 11
Pilatus 13
Luzern–Engelberg Express 19

zb

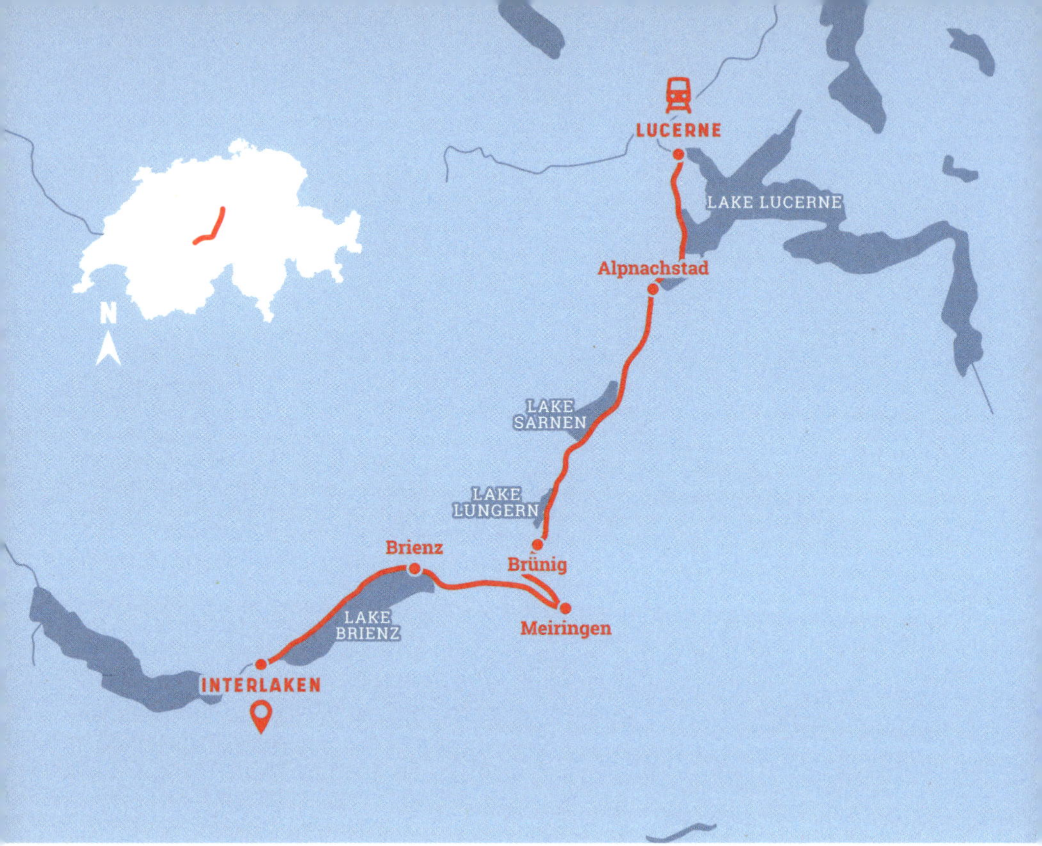

LUCERNE
LAKE LUCERNE
Alpnachstad
LAKE SARNEN
LAKE LUNGERN
Brienz
Brünig
Meiringen
LAKE BRIENZ
INTERLAKEN
N

Brünig
1000 m
900 m
800 m
700 m
600 m
500 m
400 m
LUCERNE
Alpnachstad
Meiringen
Brienz
INTERLAKEN

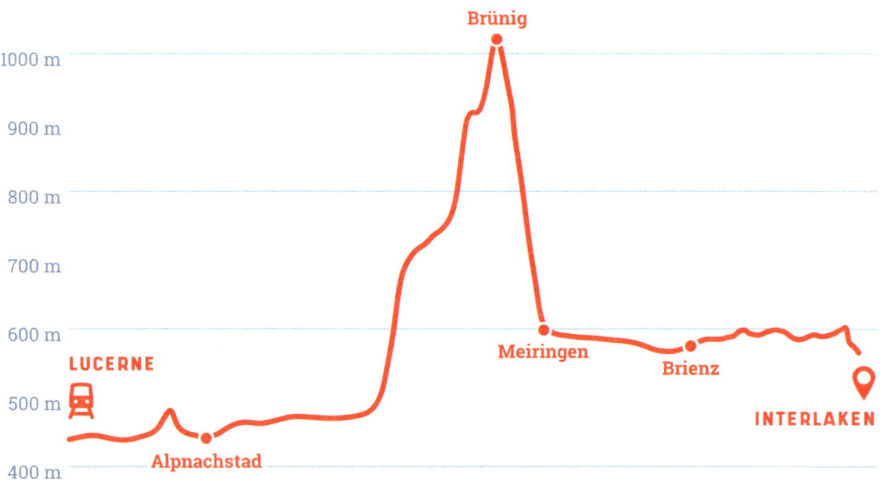

THE ROUTE

As the train leaves Lucerne, the lake is on the left but don't be fooled – the best views are on the right the rest of the way. That's clear at pretty Lake Sarnen with perfect reflections when the water is calm. After that, the railway starts its climb to reach the next lake, Lake Lungern, which was once bigger but then partially drained to create much-needed new farmland.

Now the line rises quite steeply and is single track for most of the way, with places for the downhill train to pass. Lofty peaks, such as Wilerhorn, dominate the green valley while the road twists and turns alongside the railway until both reach the Brünig Pass. The old station is a popular antique shop, so I often get off to look around before catching the next train one hour later. A slow descent from the pass reveals the wide flat Aare valley framed by high cliffs, ribbon-like waterfalls and a ridge of jagged mountains.

Before going to Lake Brienz, the train diverts to Meiringen, once an essential detour for the line to succeed both politically and economically. Here, we reverse direction but don't move! The same side (now the left) lets you enjoy the opaque turquoise waters of Switzerland's deepest lake all the way to Interlaken.

The narrow passage through the Brünig Pass opened in 1888.

THE HISTORY

On 14 June 1888 the Brünig Line opened with great fanfare and six trains a day run by its creators, the Jura-Bern-Luzern railway. Except at the start, it didn't reach either Lucerne or Interlaken but merely the lake beside each town. Passengers had to travel by steamship from Lucerne to Alpnachstad, where they could board the train and then, once in Brienz, change to another boat to reach Interlaken. Using the lakes at each end reduced the work needed to build the line but made the original travel time about six hours. You can still take boats at the beginning and end, but use the train between Alpnachstad and Brienz.

The first improvement came with the Lopper Tunnel in 1889, linking Lucerne with Alpnachstad, but the final lakeshore section from Brienz to Interlaken was only completed in August 1916. Finally, this lovely narrow-gauge line could run all the way from start to finish and all year round – it originally ran only in summer. What had initially been seen as a strategic route to connect Bern with the Gotthard (its one-metre gauge proved unsuitable for cargo trains), the Brünig Line quickly became a railway that was, and still is, sustained by tourism. Today it's operated by the Zentralbahn, an independent subsidiary of SBB.

TRIP TIPS

One year younger than the Brünig Line is the impressively dramatic train line up to the top of Mt Pilatus. Get off at Alpnachstad if you want to have the wow factor of travelling on the world's steepest cog railway.

South of Lake Sarnen in Obwalden is the geographical centre of Switzerland, at a place called Älggialp. You can only reach the exact point (46° 48′ 4″N, 8° 13′ 36″E) on foot though you can drive most of the way from Sachseln.

Meiringen is not only the supposed birthplace of the meringue (hence the name) but also where Sherlock Holmes 'died', at the Reichenbach Falls on the edge of town. Ride the historic funicular up beside the falls to see the precise spot.

11 BRIENZER ROTHORN

Historic steam rack railway with splendid views that is still delighting passengers after more than 130 years.

There's something really rather special about sitting in an open-sided carriage, looking down on a turquoise lake and hearing the puff of a steam engine. The Brienz Rothorn Railway has a unique place as the last steam mountain train in Switzerland, and I love it. Trains only run from June to October, and get very busy at times, but the views and the engines make this trip more than memorable.

Apart from the scenery, the eight steam engines are the main attraction. Two are original from 1891–92 and two are from the 1930s – all requiring a crew of three, 300kg of coal and 2000 litres of water for a return journey. The four steam engines from the 1990s are oil-fired, need only two crew and can carry twice as many passengers. There are also three diesel engines, used in peak periods so always check if the train you book is a steam one.

FAST FACTS

START
Brienz

DISTANCE
7.6km

HEIGHT DIFFERENCE
1676m

PASSES
GA, Swiss Travel Pass & Half Fare card: 50% discount

END
Brienzer Rothorn

TIME NEEDED
55min

WHERE TO SIT
On the left going uphill

NEARBY LINES
Luzern–Interlaken Express 10
Jungfraujoch 12
The Lötschberger 17

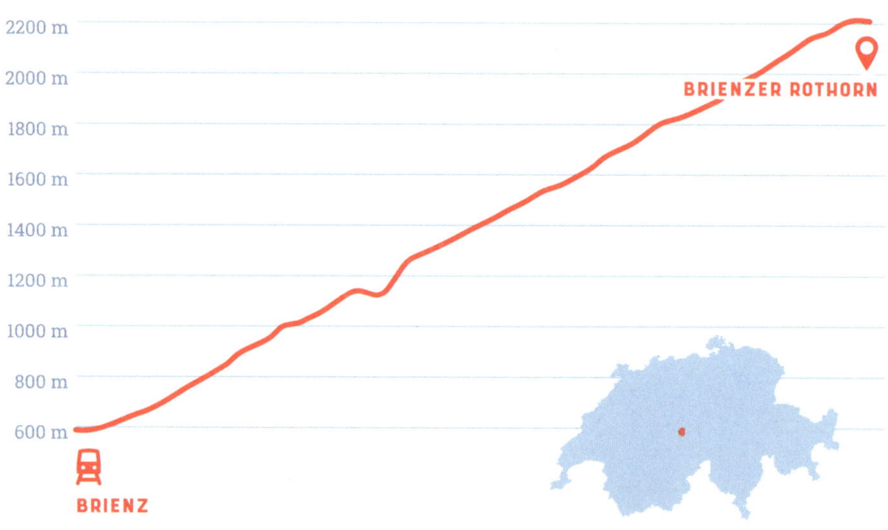
2200 m
2000 m
1800 m
1600 m
1400 m
1200 m
1000 m
800 m
600 m
BRIENZER ROTHORN
BRIENZ

THE ROUTE

Once the engine has built up enough steam, it slowly chugs out of the lakeside station, pushing the red carriages uphill – pushing rather than pulling so that it can cope with the maximum gradient of 25% and heavy carriages full of people. At first it's all trees with only glimpses of the lake but that soon changes, so sit on the left.

The big reveal comes as you're going through Schwarzfluh and Planalpfluh tunnels, thanks to giant windows cut into the rock: it's a picture-perfect view of the vibrantly coloured lake far below. On upwards to the halfway point at Planalp, where more water is taken on board for the final push – and very often Alp cheese is on sale from a local farmer.

Above the tree line, the landscape opens out to reveal Alpine meadows, often dotted with cows, or also chamois on the rocky slopes above. As the train curls round behind a sharp ridge, the whole panorama of lake and mountains is on the left. Once at the top station, take the short hike to the summit (2348m) for the 360° view of 693 peaks, including Säntis in the east and the Eiger in the west. Simply stunning.

THE HISTORY

This 1949 poster by Brienz artist Adolf Gander even has a tiny steam train.

It's not easy being the last steam mountain railway in Switzerland but the Brienz Rothorn Railway has often had to overcome seemingly impossible challenges – although things looked good at the beginning. Soon after the federal concession was granted in December 1889, construction began, involving around 700 workers, mainly from Italy. The railway was completed in 16 months and opened on 16 June 1892. But things went downhill for the rack railway as low passenger numbers, high running costs and a bad economic climate led to annual deficits.

The railway was mothballed during the First World War but then saved by the people of Brienz and recommissioned in 1931. Ironically, that time out of action and lack of money meant it was never electrified so steam survived. But it couldn't compete with modern aerial cable cars – in 1958 it was decided to demolish the line. Saved again at the last minute, it has survived and thrived ever since, mainly thanks to a patrons' association that supports the running and renovations of the line. It faced another huge challenge when a violent storm in August 2024 wrecked large sections of the tracks, requiring around five million Swiss francs for the reconstruction.

TRIP TIPS

For the complete steam adventure, I love to arrive in Brienz by paddle-steamer and switch straight to the rack railway. The boat trip from Interlaken takes about an hour and a quarter (far longer than the 20 minutes on the train), with the elegant paddle-steamer 'Lötschberg' (pictured below) running twice a day in summer.

This is a very popular train, especially on sunny days in the peak summer period when almost every departure can be sold out. I would book a ticket with a guaranteed seat in advance so that you're sure to get on board. By the way, you can travel free on your birthday.

A very special experience is to stay overnight in the small hotel at the top of the railway. Wood-panelled bedrooms are rustic but chic with comfy beds and in-room sinks, though bathrooms are shared. Prices include a buffet breakfast and, of course, plenty of fresh air.

12 JUNGFRAUJOCH

Spectacular and dramatic, the trip up to the highest train station in Europe is an unforgettable experience.

Nowhere else in Europe can you take a train up to 3454m above sea level. In just over two hours you chug ever upwards from lowly Interlaken to the final station at Jungfraujoch. Not only that, but you tunnel up inside the Eiger and emerge on a ridge overlooking the Aletsch Glacier. It is a breathtaking ride – literally, as at that high altitude the air is much thinner. No wonder it's known as the Top of Europe.

This journey from Interlaken requires taking trains on three different lines, all with their own names although they're run by the same company. This chapter is divided into three sections, one per line, as each of them is a great train trip in its own right. You can enjoy the first leg as the best way to reach the Jungfrau Region, or add the second stage for the mountain drama of Kleine Scheidegg. Or go the whole hog up to the dizzying heights of Jungfraujoch.

FAST FACTS

START
Interlaken

END
Jungfraujoch

DISTANCE
32km

TIME NEEDED
2h 7min

HEIGHT DIFFERENCE
2887m

WHERE TO SIT
On the right

PASSES
GA & Swiss Travel Pass: variable validity; Half Fare card: 50% discount

NEARBY LINES
Luzern–Interlaken Express 10
Schynige Platte 15
Grütschalp–Mürren 18

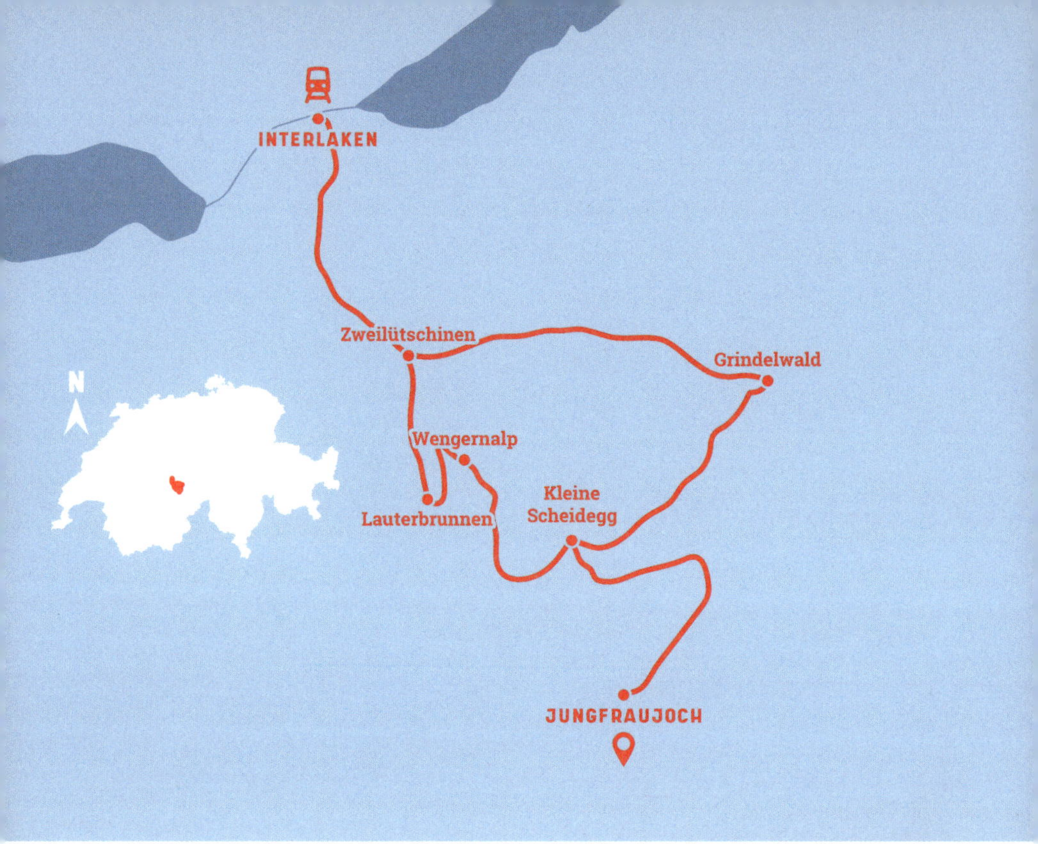

INTERLAKEN
Zweilütschinen
Grindelwald
N
Wengernalp
Lauterbrunnen
Kleine
Scheidegg
JUNGFRAUJOCH

JUNGFRAUJOCH
3500 m
3000 m
2500 m
Kleine
Scheidegg
2000 m
Via Lauterbrunnen
1500 m
Via Grindelwald
Grindelwald
1000 m
INTERLAKEN
Lauterbrunnen
Zweilütschinen
500 m

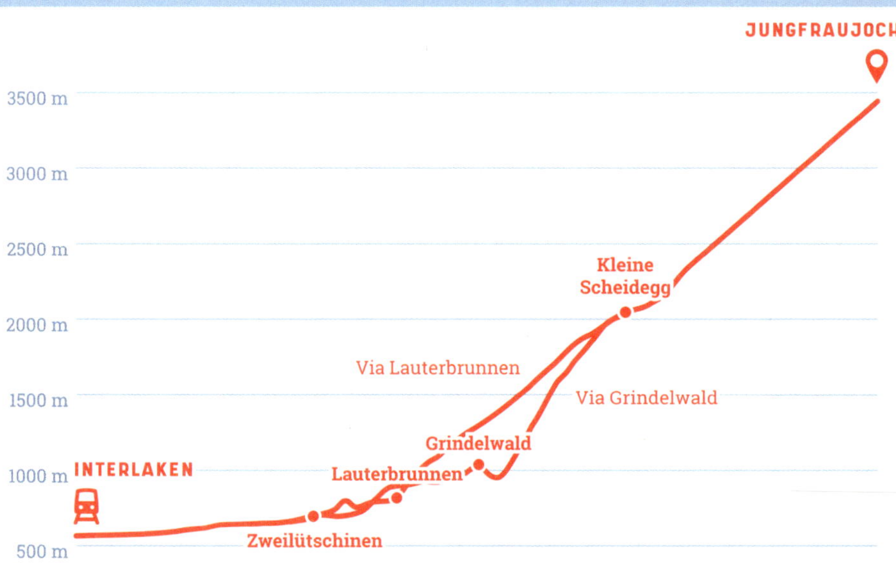

TRIP TIPS

The route to Kleine Scheidegg, where you change trains for the last leg, is a loop, so can be done in either direction. I prefer going anti-clockwise: up via Lauterbrunnen and down via Grindelwald as the views are more impressive, especially for first-timers. But either direction is truly memorable.

There is now a quicker way to or from the top – the Eiger Express. This swish new cable car between Grindelwald and Eigergletscher cuts out 45 minutes of slow train travel, so is ideal if you're in a hurry. I still prefer taking the original railway but the price is the same so you could hop on the Express one way to save time.

Tickets are a little more complicated than usual. The GA, the Swiss Travel Pass and day passes are only valid to Grindelwald or Wengen. After that, it's 50% discount for the GA, 25% for the Swiss Travel Pass and nothing for day passes. The Half Fare card is 50% all the way. Reservations are highly recommended for the final leg to Jungfraujoch, especially in the busy summer months when trains are full.

BERNESE OBERLAND RAILWAY

The first stage is on the Bernese Oberland Railway (or BOB to its friends), a Y-shaped line starting in Interlaken Ost. Make sure you're in the correct part of the train, as it splits along the route.

THE ROUTE

At first it's all very gentle as the train trundles across the flat plain around Interlaken. After Wilderswil the slow climb into the mountains begins. The line enters the dramatically narrow Lütschine valley, where it promptly splits, with each half following its respective river arm: 'Schwarze Lütschine' to Grindelwald and 'Weisse Lütschine' to Lauterbrunnen.

Going anti-clockwise means heading to Lauterbrunnen first, and the further you go, the more dramatic it gets. The Lauterbrunnen Valley is justifiably an Instagram star – its deep U-shape of sheer cliffs, lush valley floor and 72 waterfalls making it one of Switzerland's natural wonders. It's a physical geography lesson come to life, and also the inspiration for Tolkien's elven realm of Rivendell.

Alternatively, sit in the back of the BOB train, which takes the left-hand fork in the river up to Grindelwald. It's a slightly longer journey, partly because the train has to climb up an extra 237m of elevation. As the landscape opens out, you get wider views of the valley, dominated by peaks like craggy Wetterhorn or the mighty Eiger itself. Sit on the right so you can look straight up the forbidding North Face.

THE HISTORY

Even after electrification, steam trains were used sometimes, as this photo from 1955 shows.

Once the train arrived in Interlaken in 1872, it was only a matter of time before the railways started snaking their way up into the mountains. Visitors wanted to see the grandeur of the Swiss landscape, so train lines were built to take them there, starting with the Berner Oberland Railway. After a failed first attempt in 1873, a new plan was made for a one-metre gauge line, with sections of cog railway to tackle the steeper gradients of up to 12%. On 1 July 1890 the BOB opened with regular services along its 23.7km from Interlaken Ost to Grindelwald and Lauterbrunnen.

The BOB line has always had its signature Y shape with the two trains coupled until separation at Zweilütschinen. But although the plan has stayed the same, changes have taken place. Electrification came in 1914, thanks to the power plants built for the railway to Jungfraujoch. Then the original brown-and-cream carriages had a makeover in 2004: the new colours of blue and yellow represent water and sunlight respectively. Some things, however, never change. Unsuspecting tourists are often in the wrong half of the train so must dash along the platform at Zweilütschinen.

WENGERNALP RAILWAY

The world's longest cogwheel railway is one of the most scenic lines in Switzerland, with splendid views of the Bernese Alps during the long, slow climb to Kleine Scheidegg at 2061m.

THE ROUTE

From Lauterbrunnen the line climbs steeply up, giving you grandstand views of this deep glacial valley and its many waterfalls. As the train curls round to gain altitude, make sure you're on the right for best photos. The first money shot comes just before Wengen with a perfect panorama of the famous valley. It's even more stunning from Wengernalp onwards, so sit in a carriage with windows that open and get your camera ready.

At Kleine Scheidegg everyone has to change trains, with most people continuing up to Jungfraujoch. The tracks of the Wengernalp Railway run through to Grindelwald but the trains don't, so a change is required. This is a busy spot in the shadow of the Eiger, with hotels, restaurants, shops and (usually) lots of people: hikers in summer, skiers in winter.

For the downhill trip to Grindelwald the left-hand side is marginally better, with widescreen views of the village in its bowl-shaped valley and mountains framing the whole scene. The train passes directly under the new Eiger Express cable car (which is a faster way down) and on through bucolic fields dotted with chalets. Stay on until the final stop to connect to the BOB line.

THE HISTORY

Even before the Bernese Oberland Railway was officially opened, plans were afoot to extend the railway up to Kleine Scheidegg. In June 1890, Leo Heer-Bétrix won the concession to build a new 19.1km-long cogwheel line from Lauterbrunnen across to Grindelwald. Construction began quickly, using the same company (Pümpin & Herzog) that was building the rack railway to Schynige Platte at that time. Both lines were built using the same narrow gauge with a rack system that had been patented by Swiss engineer Niklaus Riggenbach. By the summer of 1892 the first trains had reached Kleine Scheidegg, and public services began on 20 June 1893.

It was such an immediate success that additional trains were bought to cope with the unexpected demand ... but there was a problem. The route from Lauterbrunnen to Wengen was rather steep (a 25% gradient) and exposed to rock falls – limiting capacity and efficiency. An alternative route was built, one that was longer but not as steep, and that new line opened in 1910, to coincide with electrifying the whole railway. Today's more modern trains can travel at up to 28 km/h, which is quite fast for a cog railway.

A colourful poster by François Gos, first published in 1922.

JUNGFRAU RAILWAY

The final leg of the three-part journey to Jungfraujoch is the shortest but perhaps the most remarkable – not for the views (most of the trip is in a tunnel) but for the mammoth achievement of building the line at all.

THE ROUTE

As the sleek red carriages leave Kleine Scheidegg the views are on the right. They're fantastically grand but short-lived. After the first stop at Eigergletscher (where the Eiger Express cable car arrives), the train disappears into the tunnel. Apart from a short sightseeing stop at Eismeer, where everyone gets off to peek at the glacier, the rest of the journey is inside the mountain.

Then, 26 minutes later, you disembark at Jungfraujoch, Europe's highest train station at 3454m. Take your time, take deep breaths and take a tour of this high-altitude spot. I love the outdoor platform for the breathtaking views of rock and ice, and the multimedia show about the construction is good. But this train trip isn't really about what's at the top, as great as that is; it's about the trip itself and what it took to realise it. This triumph of Swiss engineering still seems remarkable over 100 years later.

THE HISTORY

The breakthrough at Eismeer in 1903.

It was a Sunday in August 1893 when Adolf Guyer-Zeller was hiking above Mürren with his daughter. Across the deep cleft of the Lauterbrunnen Valley, he could see a train chugging its way up the Wengernalp Railway, barely two months after its inauguration. That's when he decided to build a railway to the top of the Jungfrau. He was granted the concession and construction began on 27 July 1896.

The monumental undertaking involved digging a tunnel up inside the Eiger but Guyer-Zeller cleverly chose to open the line in stages. Each new stop along the way became a tourist attraction – Eigergletscher was the first in 1898 – with ticket sales helping to finance the project. But his death in 1899 and tight finances meant that the original plans were changed. The summit of the Jungfrau was no longer the goal but instead the outcrop of rock at Jungfraujoch.

It would take 16 years and 16 million francs to complete the Jungfrau Railway, and it was tough work: 30 men died building this 7.3km tunnel. Finally on 1 August 1912, the first train took passengers all the way up to Jungfraujoch. Back then the journey time was 1¼ hours (compared to 26 minutes today), but at least it was an electric line from the start, so no steam and soot filled the long tunnel.

13 PILATUS

The steepest cog railway in the world is a wonder for its technological achievement and spectacular views.

As engineering marvels of the 19th century go, building the world's steepest railway in just 400 days of labour must be up there with the best. Conquering the vertiginous gradients seemed like an impossible challenge but it was achieved with some creative thinking. And thank goodness for that because we can still enjoy the results of this triumph of science today. This is not a long trip but it's certainly worth it, not least for the 360° panorama from the top.

The Pilatus railway only operates from May to November, so can get rather busy at peak times, such as sunny weekends. Seat reservations are not obligatory but highly recommended to avoid queuing when it might be crowded. You can of course travel in either direction but I prefer going uphill to experience the effect of the maximum gradient of 48%. For the full Pilatus experience, get the Golden Round Trip Ticket, which also includes the boat from Lucerne plus cable car and bus to get back.

FAST FACTS

START
Alpnachstad

END
Pilatus Kulm

DISTANCE
4.6km

TIME NEEDED
27min

HEIGHT DIFFERENCE
1635m

WHERE TO SIT
On the left going uphill

PASSES
GA, Swiss Travel Pass & Half Fare card: 50% discount

NEARBY LINES
Luzern–Interlaken Express 10
Rigi 14
Voralpen-Express 29

PILATUS
43

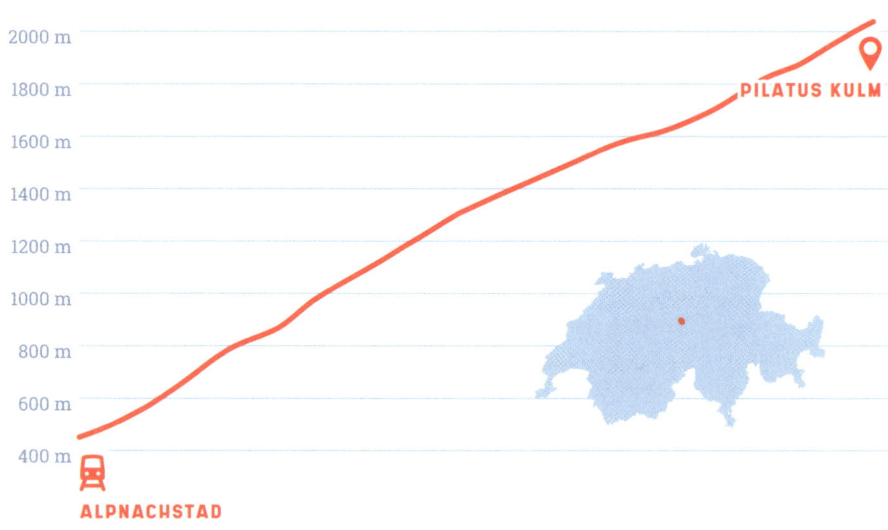
2000 m
1800 m
1600 m
1400 m
1200 m
1000 m
800 m
600 m
400 m
PILATUS KULM
ALPNACHSTAD

THE ROUTE

Alpnachstad sits at the end of one finger of Lake Lucerne and you get there by suburban train or boat, depending on whether you choose speed or scenery. Either way, you end up at the start of the cog railway with its sleek red carriages waiting at an incredible incline.

As soon as you set off, you feel how steep the slope is. Luckily, the train is cleverly designed so that you're not constantly sliding forwards or backwards – and the new carriages inaugurated in 2023 have comfy seats and huge windows. At first you climb slowly but steadily through the forest, with the glimpses of blue water gradually getting more distant.

After the halfway stop (where the up and down trains cross) the landscape opens up in dramatic fashion: sit on the left for the best views. If you thought Pilatus looked craggy from Lucerne, wait until you see how rugged it is up close. And yet the train trundles on upwards past the sheer rocky outcrops, and sometimes through them. Finally, it glides into the Kulm station at 2070m above sea level.

THE HISTORY

The world's steepest cog railway was steam powered for the first 48 years.

On 4 June 1889 the first passenger train chugged up to Pilatus Kulm. In those days the steam train travelled at the stately speed of 3.6 km/h and took 70 minutes to get uphill (compared to 15 km/h and 27 minutes today). But that the railway existed at all was nothing short of a wonder, and it was all down to the Swiss engineer Eduard Locher. He devised the revolutionary horizontal double cogwheel system that allowed the train to conquer the steep gradients – with the help of almost 54,000 pairs of teeth along the track.

It was a storming success from day one. Built for 15,000 passengers a year, the railway carried over 36,000 passengers in the first six months alone. And that despite the price: an uphill ticket in 1899 cost 10 Swiss francs, or equivalent to one week's wages for a normal worker. Despite this popularity, the steam trains were heavy and slow, needing 300kg of coal for a return journey, so the line was electrified in 1937. Shorter journey times and bigger carriages meant even more people could go up Pilatus.

TRIP TIPS

If you take the Golden Round Trip, do it clockwise from Lucerne. That way you arrive by boat, go uphill on the cog railway then take the scenic cable car back down. The main drawback is that it's more popular so to avoid any potential queues, start early or instead go round anti-clockwise.

Make time for some scenic hikes at the summit. The best views of Lucerne and its lake are from Esel, a short but steep climb up from the Kulm station. The longer hike to Tomlishorn (around 90 minutes return) takes you to the highest point on the mountain at 2132m.

For an unforgettable experience, stay overnight in the elegant Pilatus-Kulm Hotel, built in 1890. After the day-trippers have gone, peacefully watch the fiery sunset then have supper in the grand dining room. On clear nights, you can see the Milky Way before waking up for a sunrise with ibex grazing nearby.

14 RIGI

Europe's oldest mountain railway is still going strong and the views are as impressive as they've always been.

Once upon a time watching the sunrise from the top of Rigi was the absolute must-do for visitors to Switzerland. It was so popular that the Swiss built Europe's first mountain train to take more people up more quickly. Today, most tourists just come for the day, using that same historic line to enjoy the superb panorama of lakes and mountains. But you can still stay overnight, and the sunrise still happens every day, and it's a serene Swiss moment you'll never forget.

There are two routes to the top, one line from Vitznau, the other from Arth-Goldau. This odd situation is a historic hangover from when two train companies from two cantons competed to reach the 1797m summit. But it does mean you can make a perfect round trip: a boat from Lucerne to Vitznau for the dramatic journey uphill, then back down the other side to Arth-Goldau to connect to the main line.

FAST FACTS

START
Vitznau

DISTANCE
6.9km

HEIGHT DIFFERENCE
1317m

PASSES
GA & Swiss Travel Pass: free;
Half Fare card: 50% discount

END
Rigi Kulm

TIME NEEDED
32min

WHERE TO SIT
On the left

NEARBY LINES
Pilatus 13
Gotthard Railway 26
Voralpen-Express 29

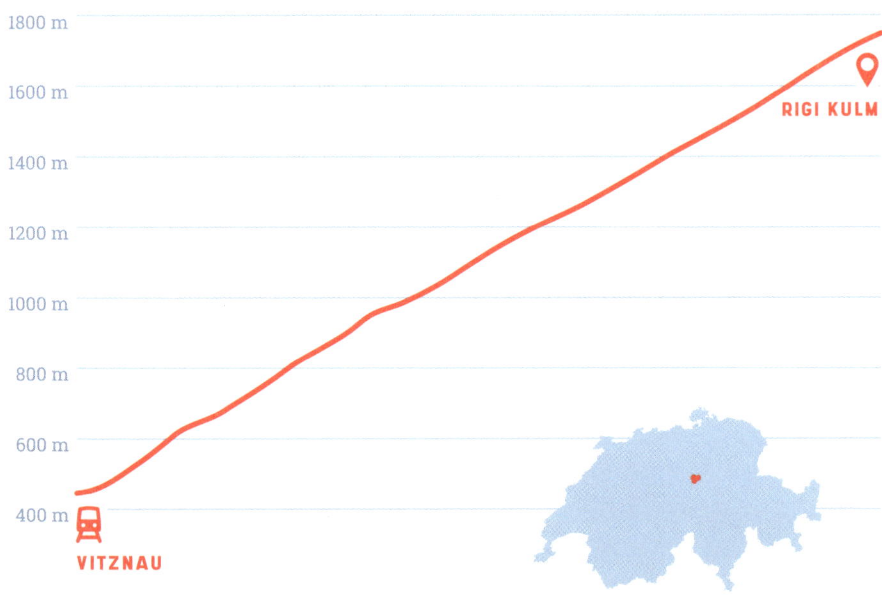
1800 m
1600 m
1400 m
1200 m
1000 m
800 m
600 m
400 m
RIGI KULM
VITZNAU

THE ROUTE

Boat and train are perfectly in synch in Vitznau so a few minutes after disembarking from the former, you're sitting in the swish new carriages of the Rigi Bahn. Then it's a slow steady climb up behind the church and between the houses until the village is left behind. Snatches of blue water appear on the left between dark fir trees but then, as if by magic, the whole lake is revealed in one glorious moment.

A few hundred metres higher and you cross the cantonal border between Lucerne and Schwyz (although the top of Rigi is squarely in the latter). At Staffel, the blue-and-white trains from Arth-Goldau arrive, with both then continuing up to the Kulm station at 1752m. For the final 45 metres to the summit, you have to walk but it's worth the short steep climb from behind the hotel.

Standing on top, surrounded by lakes and mountains, you really can grasp why countless thousands of people have come up here over the years: the 'Queen of the Mountains' reigns supreme over central Switzerland with her 360° panorama. From Titlis to the Eiger and Pilatus, the Alps dominate the horizon while glittering water sits way down below you. It's a picture-perfect view that seems too wonderful to be real.

THE HISTORY

This poster from 1920 included a timetable for reaching Rigi via Arth-Goldau.

It's a hearty hike up to Rigi Kulm but thousands used to do it – or, if you were rich, get carried up in a sedan chair as Queen Victoria once was. So many potential customers made the financial incentive for a railway large enough that two were built in competition, each backed by its own canton. Lucerne won this railway race, with its line from Vitznau opening on 21 May 1871, though it only reached the cantonal border at Staffelhöhe. The final section to the summit opened on 27 June 1873, built by Schwyz and then rented out to Lucerne to help finance its own line.

Coming up the back side of Rigi, the Schwyz line from Arth-Goldau wasn't finished until 1875 but that was still early enough to cash in on the railway boom. In the first summer alone, 60,000 people took the train from Vitznau, even though the steam trains were small and slow. Rigi quickly became the tourist centre of Switzerland, with grand hotels built for the flood of visitors wanting to ride the then-unique railway. Both lines were built on a standard gauge of 1435mm and used Niklaus Riggenbach's ingenious rack system, but they continued to be run as separate companies until a merger in 1992.

TRIP TIPS

Wear your walking boots because Rigi has plenty of great hikes. My favourites are from Rigi Kulm down to Kaltbad and then on out to Känzeli, or the 7km-long Panoramaweg along the old railway line to Scheidegg.

If you want to relax after a hike, or even without any walking at all, look no further than the sleek spa at Kaltbad. Designed by Swiss star architect Mario Botta, the building is almost as beautiful as the mountain views from the outdoor pools.

Stay overnight at the comfortable Rigi Kulm Hotel and you'll have the mountain pretty much to yourself once the day-trippers have gone. Plus you can get up extra early to enjoy a truly Swiss experience: watching the sun rise from a mountain top.

15 SCHYNIGE PLATTE

Pure nostalgia on this historic mountain train with original rolling stock, wooden carriages and unbeatable views.

This isn't the highest, steepest or longest mountain train in Switzerland, but the trip to Schynige Platte is easily one of my favourites. This little train with red carriages could be straight out of a fairy tale but is often overlooked by many visitors. While they head up to nearby Jungfraujoch, the canny travellers get off the train from Interlaken at Wilderswil and switch to this blast from the past.

It feels as if almost nothing has changed since the line opened in 1893. No panorama cars or comfy upholstery, it's all wooden seats and open windows. Great for taking perfect photos, though hard on your backside. At least the journey is under an hour, using a rack railway with a maximum gradient of 25% and no electronic signals (it's all done by hand). It only runs from late May to October.

FAST FACTS

START
Wilderswil

END
Schynige Platte

DISTANCE
7.2km

TIME NEEDED
52min

HEIGHT DIFFERENCE
1381m

WHERE TO SIT
On the right going uphill

PASSES
GA, Swiss Travel Pass & Half Fare card: 50% discount

NEARBY LINES
GoldenPass Line 1
Jungfraujoch 12
Grütschalp–Mürren 18

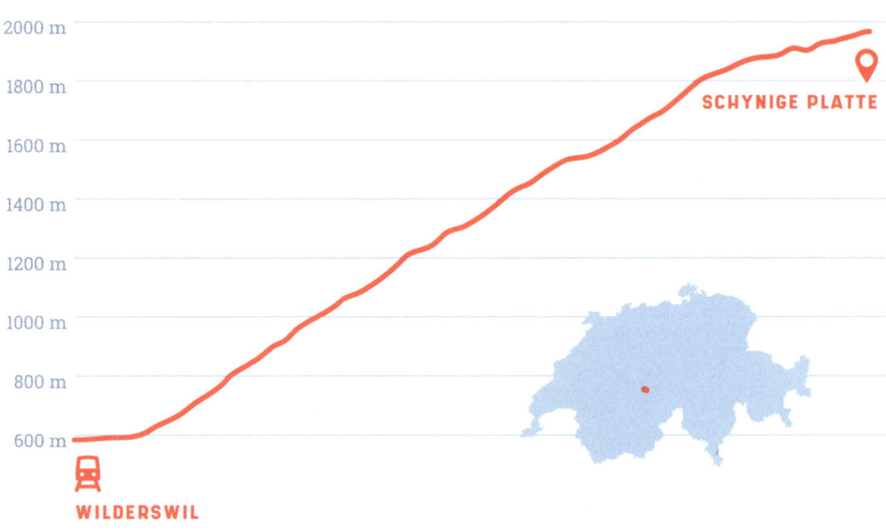
2000 m
1800 m
1600 m
1400 m
1200 m
1000 m
800 m
600 m
SCHYNIGE PLATTE
WILDERSWIL

THE ROUTE

After crossing the rushing torrent of the Lütschine river, the line climbs through thick forests until the landscape opens to reveal the lakes below. The best views come after the halfway stop at Breitlauenen, briefly on the left-hand side of the train but mainly on the right. As the line curls on round, there's a great shot of blue Lake Thun and the pyramidal peak of Niesen.

The wow moment comes after a short stone tunnel about two-thirds of the way up. Filling the whole right-hand side is the panorama of the Eiger, Mönch and Jungfrau mountains.

Expect an audible intake of breath from first-timers and furious photo snapping from everyone. It's a view that never fails to impress.

Schynige Platte translates literally as 'shining plates', referring to the dark slate that glistens in the sun, especially after a rain shower. But people come for the views not the slate. The peaks of the Bernese Oberland are easily seen from the end station, at 1967m above sea level, or the nearby restaurant terrace. With a backdrop like that, it's no wonder this is extremely popular in high summer.

THE HISTORY

This wonderful line was built in only two summers – in 1891 and 1892 – which is a remarkably short time given the logistics of the landscape. It's over 7km from Wilderswil to the top, with 67 bends, four tunnels and a height difference of almost 1400m. Despite all that, the tracks and stations were built quickly, so that on 15 May 1893 the first invited guests chugged up to Schynige Platte at a top speed of 10 km/h. Scheduled passenger services began a month later.

The final cost of building the line, including the trains and stations, came to 3.5 million Swiss francs. That was more than half a million over budget, and quite a tidy sum in the 1890s. More costs came with electrification in 1914 but the modern trains made the journey faster and cleaner. The atmospheric steam engine No. 5 is still used occasionally but the old open-air carriages are in service every summer. As the line isn't in use all year, the electric cables and masts are taken down each autumn and put up again in the spring.

Iconic 1932 poster by Alex Walter Diggelmann.

TRIP TIPS

The ultimate 360° panorama needs a bit of legwork. It's a steep 20-minute walk from Schynige Platte station up to the Daube viewpoint but the effort is rewarded with a spectacular aerial view of Interlaken and its two lakes, plus all the mountains around. Wear good shoes for this rocky walk, especially if you carry on along the even more impressive panorama hike (about 2½ hours).

One alternative for the return journey is to hike halfway down to the middle station at Breitlauenen: it takes around 1½ hours with a height difference of 425m. The views are wonderful the whole way, especially if you want pictures of the train as it trundles past.

For the real Schynige Platte experience, stay overnight in the rustic but comfortable hotel. It isn't the height of luxury (rooms have shared bathrooms) but with views like this, who cares. Once the day-trippers have gone, the fabulous sunsets can be enjoyed in peace.

16 BERN ↔ LUCERNE

Relaxed ride along the scenic route through the rounded hills and cow-filled fields of the Emmental and Entlebuch.

This could easily be known as the slow train through Switzerland, a calm comfortable alternative to the main line connection between Bern and Lucerne. Geographically, it's the more direct route between the two cities but takes half an hour longer than travelling on the SBB line to the north. And it's certainly the more scenic option, passing through a delightful rural kaleidoscope of big-roofed farmhouses, gentle hills, small towns and lots of cows. Really, lots of cows.

The meandering route is divided between two river valleys and two cantons. On the Canton Lucerne side is the Entlebuch, a Unesco Biosphere Reserve of protected natural landscape along the Kleine Emme River. Over in Canton Bern, the railway travels through the Emmental, named after the River Emme and in turn giving its name to the famous holey cheese. The direct connection through both valleys is the hourly RegioExpress operated by BLS.

FAST FACTS

START
Bern

END
Lucerne

DISTANCE
95km

TIME NEEDED
1h 27min

HEIGHT DIFFERENCE
418m

WHERE TO SIT
On the right

PASSES
GA & Swiss Travel Pass: free;
Half Fare card: 50% discount

NEARBY LINES
Bern–Geneva 4
Luzern–Interlaken Express 10
Pilatus 13

THE ROUTE

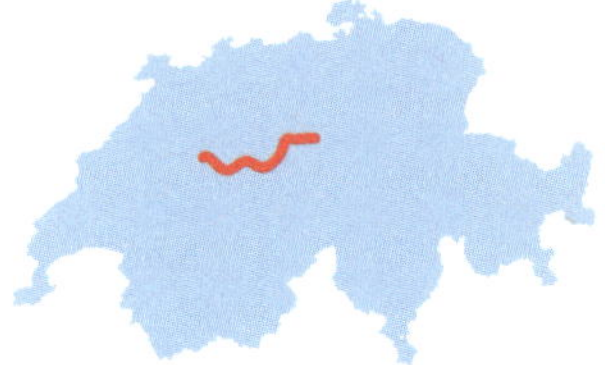

Heading south from Bern there are clear-day views of the Alps on the right, especially as the train veers east towards the Emmental, giving great views across the broad Aare Valley. Almost immediately come the first typical farmhouses with roofs the size of tennis courts. And the first cows.

The hills slowly get hillier, resembling domes of carefully-mown grass often crowned by a farmhouse or solitary tree. Past the main town, Langnau im Emmental, things get a bit wilder, with less farmland and more trees. Then my favourite stop, Trubschachen, purely for the Kambly biscuit factory to indulge in the free tastings.

The highest point of the line is at Escholzmatt (853m), with great views of low-rise mountains along the craggier skyline. Deep in the Entlebuch comes the most dramatic section, with limestone ridges, a winding river and even the cliff-top convent of Werthenstein. Finally, the built-up approach to Lucerne.

THE HISTORY

A 1946 photo of a train used to transport cattle from Schüpfheim.

This is a line born as a big idea: a railway from Bern to Zurich via Lucerne. It was the brainchild of Bruno Hildebrand, the chairman of the Swiss East-West Railway, who envisioned it as competition to the main line being built by his rival Alfred Escher. He was supported by Canton Bern to the tune of two million francs, but despite that the company went bankrupt in 1861. It was taken over by the canton to form the Bern State Railway, the first purely state-run railway in Switzerland.

Construction continued at the Bernese end of the line, so that by June 1864 trains ran from Bern to Langnau but no further. The railway through the Entlebuch from Lucerne took longer and was finally completed on 11 August 1875. It was run by the Bern Lucerne Railway, which also took over the Bernese section, but that company went into liquidation a year later. Canton Bern bought it to ensure the railway continued operating. Today the line is run by BLS.

17 THE LÖTSCHBERGER

Take the high line with the old tunnel or the low route with the new one to travel under the Bernese Alps.

The train ride between Bern and Brig is one of the unsung heroes of the Swiss rail network. Not only does it wind its way through some stunning countryside but it also cuts journey times between north and south by tunnelling under the Alps.

Without the Lötschberg line, it's a long way round via Lake Geneva, but with it Switzerland is a lot smaller, meaning that you can reach Valais, and Italy, quickly and easily.

Taking the train through the Lötschberg tunnel involves making a choice because there are two possible routes. The original line from 1913 is slower but more scenic with a shorter tunnel and more time to admire the landscape. The faster option is the main line via the new base tunnel, opened in 2007: you will see less but save time. Both routes go to Brig and then on through the Simplon Tunnel to Domodossola in Italy, where you can connect to the Centovalli Railway to Ticino.

FAST FACTS

START

Bern

END
Brig

DISTANCE
115km

TIME NEEDED
1h 42min

HEIGHT DIFFERENCE
690m

WHERE TO SIT
On the right towards Brig

PASSES

GA & Swiss Travel Pass: free;
Half Fare card: 50% discount

NEARBY LINES
Geneva–Brig 5
Centovalli Railway 20
Glacier Express 21

bls
bls
bls

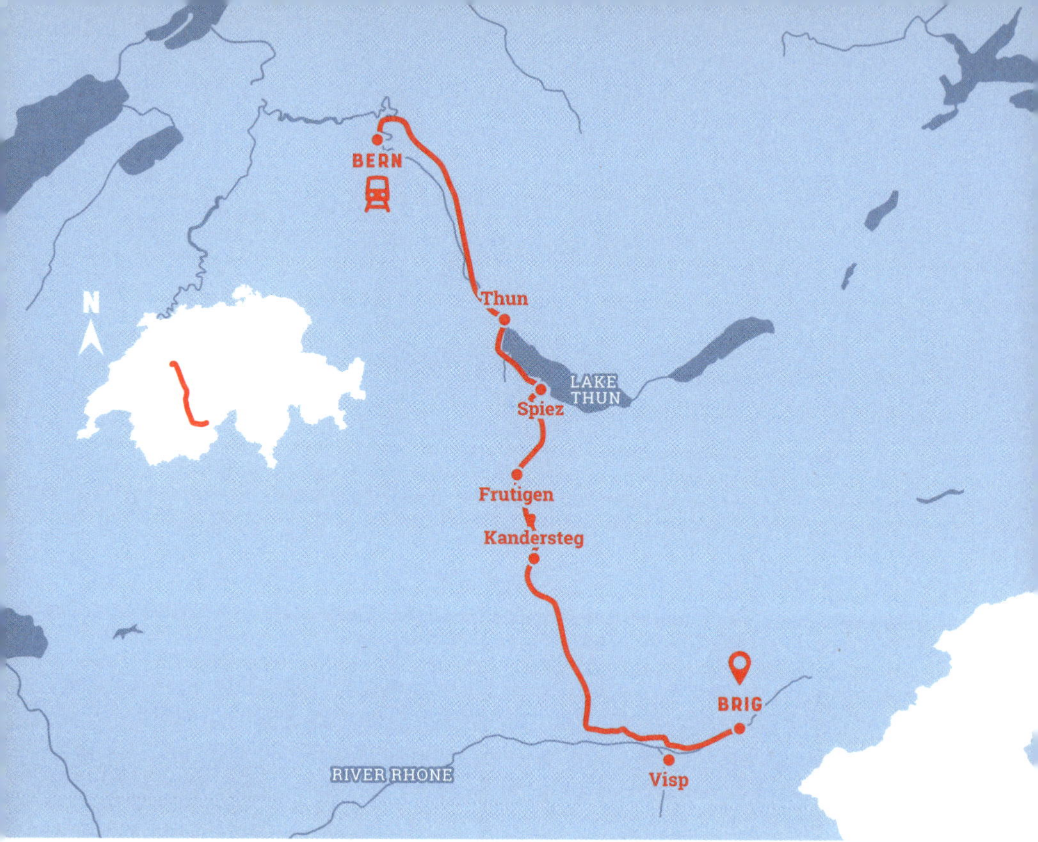

BERN
Thun
LAKE
THUN
Spiez
Frutigen
Kandersteg
BRIG
RIVER RHONE
Visp
N

1300 m
1200 m
1100 m
1000 m
900 m
800 m
700 m
600 m
500 m
BERN
Thun
Kandersteg
BRIG

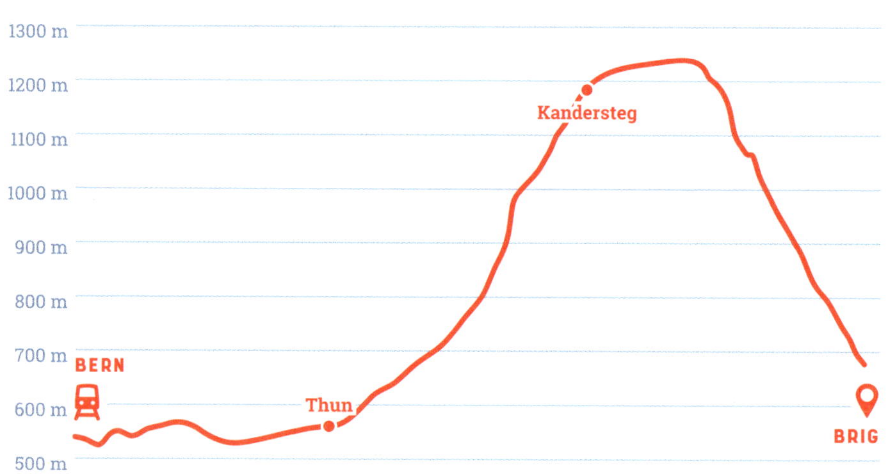

THE ROUTE

Let's take the slow train and enjoy the scenery, which starts in earnest at Thun, with its Rapunzel-like castle and glittering lake. The line follows the lakeshore on the left until Spiez, where it heads south to the mountains. Spiez is the last stop where you can switch to the fast Intercity train through the new tunnel.

After Frutigen, the train climbs steadily, with the impressive views switching between left and right as the line loops round and up to Kandersteg. The village has a prime position surrounded by rugged peaks, and is the gateway to the old tunnel. You often see vehicles being loaded into the open-sided carriages of the car transport train, the only way to 'drive' to Valais from here.

Fourteen minutes later and you're in Valais, high above the Rhone Valley. The railway line seems to cling to the rock, traversing deep ravines on towering bridges with the expansive landscape on the right-hand side. It's almost like being in a low-flying aircraft but eventually you come down to land in Brig.

THE HISTORY

Excavating the original Lötschberg Tunnel, which opened in 1913.

It took a while for this line to be built, as the railway from Bern opened in stages: 1859 the train reached Thun, 1893 Spiez and 1901 Frutigen. From there, travelling via the Lötschen Pass meant going through the Alps on foot as there was no road through to the Rhone Valley – and still isn't. All that changed with the first Lötschberg Tunnel. It was the centrepiece of a grand plan for an alternative connection between France and Italy, a direct competitor to the more central Gotthard Tunnel.

The company set up to build it was BLS (short for Bern-Simplon-Lötschberg), which still runs the hourly train service today. The 14.6km-long tunnel was dug under the pass at great cost: 52 million francs, 961 tonnes of explosives and, sadly, 64 lives. When the first passenger train ran with great fanfare on 15 July 1913, it travelled through the third-longest tunnel in Switzerland, after the Simplon and the Gotthard. Almost 100 years after the first inauguration, there was a second in June 2007 to mark the completion of the Lötschberg Base Tunnel. This new one is much longer, at 34.6km, and much pricier, a mere 4.3 billion francs, but also flatter and faster.

TRIP TIPS

Shortly after Spiez, the train passes by one of Switzerland's best, and longest, funiculars. Get off at Mülenen (it's a request stop so ring the bell) and glide up to the 2336m-high summit of Niesen, known as the Swiss Pyramid.

There are plenty of hiking opportunities between Bern and Brig. A top option is to get off at Kandersteg and go up to beautiful Lake Oeschinen. Or, after the tunnel, walk the 'south ramp' from Hohtenn to Eggerberg, following the train line with grandstand views of the Rhone.

The big advantage of taking the fast route is that you emerge from the new tunnel in Visp, where you can connect to trains to Zermatt or towards Lake Geneva. It saves an hour over the old route, making day trips to see the Matterhorn more feasible.

18 GRÜTSCHALP ↔ MÜRREN

Short but stunning narrow-gauge railway that runs along the cliffs high above Lauterbrunnen Valley.

There aren't many train lines that are only accessible by cable car but this is one of them. The only way to reach Grütschalp is by cable car from Lauterbrunnen and the only way to escape Mürren is the cable car down to Stechelberg – unless you want to hike up or down the 700m-high cliff. But that's not the only thing that makes this short line special; it also has grandstand views of the Bernese Alps so make sure you sit on the left facing forwards.

My favourite way to enjoy this unique train line is to ride the rails one way and hike back. The path runs right beside the railway so you get great views of the train with the mountains as a backdrop. It's around 90 minutes to hike the route, and the path is also open in winter. If hiking isn't your thing, then make a circuit, returning from Mürren via the cable car to Stechelberg, then the Postbus back to Lauterbrunnen. Or simply enjoy the train trip in reverse.

FAST FACTS

START
Grütschalp

DISTANCE
4.3km

HEIGHT DIFFERENCE
152m

PASSES
GA & Swiss Travel Pass: free;
Half Fare card: 50% discount

END
Mürren

TIME NEEDED
14min

WHERE TO SIT
On the left towards Mürren

NEARBY LINES
Luzern–Interlaken Express 10
Jungfraujoch 12
Schynige Platte 15

THE ROUTE

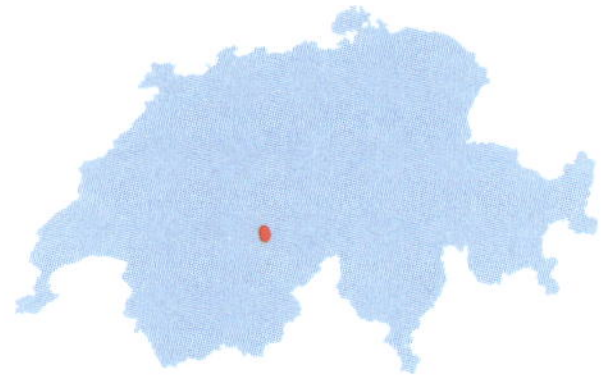

After the drama of the cable car ride up from Lauterbrunnen, you might think nothing can top that. But you ain't seen nothing yet. On busy summer days, it can be a bit crowded in the tiny Grüstchalp station but try and bag a seat on the left because the memorable views start immediately.

The big three of the Bernese Oberland – Eiger, Mönch and Jungfrau – are centre stage for practically the whole journey, only disappearing when the train goes behind the tall trees. This really is a panorama train ride to remember, with uninterrupted views across the deep valley to Wengen and those famous mountains.

This single-track railway has a crossing point at Winteregg, which has a great restaurant and terrace to enjoy those views with an ice cream or plate of Rösti. The closer you get to Mürren, the more the mountains fill the picture – it's almost impossible to look away, and a view that never gets old, no matter how many times you see it.

THE HISTORY

Historic photo from the summer of 1891, the year the railway opened.

Mürren's popularity as a summer resort meant that this was one of the earliest tourist trains to be built. Built as a metre-gauge railway with a maximum gradient of 5%, it opened on 14 August 1891. Despite being a high-altitude line (Grütschalp is at 1487m), it was electrified from the start, at that time only the third railway in Switzerland to operate with electricity. In 1903 the first winter guests arrived in Mürren and that eventually led to a year-round service in 1910.

The line's official name is the Bergbahn Lauterbrunnen-Mürren (or BLM for short), even though it's not a rack railway, so the carriages from the 1960s still have BLM on the side. It originally included a steep funicular from Lauterbrunnen to Grüstchalp but that became unstable and was replaced with the current cable car in 2006. The line is now owned by Jungfrau Railways, and new trains were inaugurated in 2024.

19 LUZERN–ENGELBERG EXPRESS

Narrow-gauge line from Lake Lucerne to the foot of one of the most popular Swiss mountains, Titlis.

This railway is not very long (only 25km) and not very wide (just one metre) but it more than makes up for that with its views of central Switzerland. Short and sweet it may be, but it's also often rather busy despite leading to a dead end – or more likely because of that dead end. Engelberg is a much-visited Alpine resort, not only for hiking in summer and skiing in winter but also for the peaks on its doorstep.

From the clear blue waters of Lake Lucerne to the bright white summit of Titlis, this is a journey designed for those who love the Swiss countryside. There's a panorama car in First Class but even from the cheap seats in Second Class, it won't disappoint. And to think, this line almost didn't survive when it came close to bankruptcy over 60 years ago: it was rescued by one of the three cantons that it passes through.

FAST FACTS

START
Lucerne

END
Engelberg

DISTANCE
25km

TIME NEEDED
43min

HEIGHT DIFFERENCE
563m

WHERE TO SIT
On the right towards Engelberg

PASSES
GA & Swiss Travel Pass: free;
Half Fare card: 50% discount

NEARBY LINES
Pilatus 13
Bern–Lucerne 16
Gotthard Railway 26

LUCERNE
LAKE LUCERNE
N
Stansstad
ENGELBERG

1000 m
900 m
800 m
700 m
600 m
500 m
400 m
LUCERNE
Stansstad
ENGELBERG

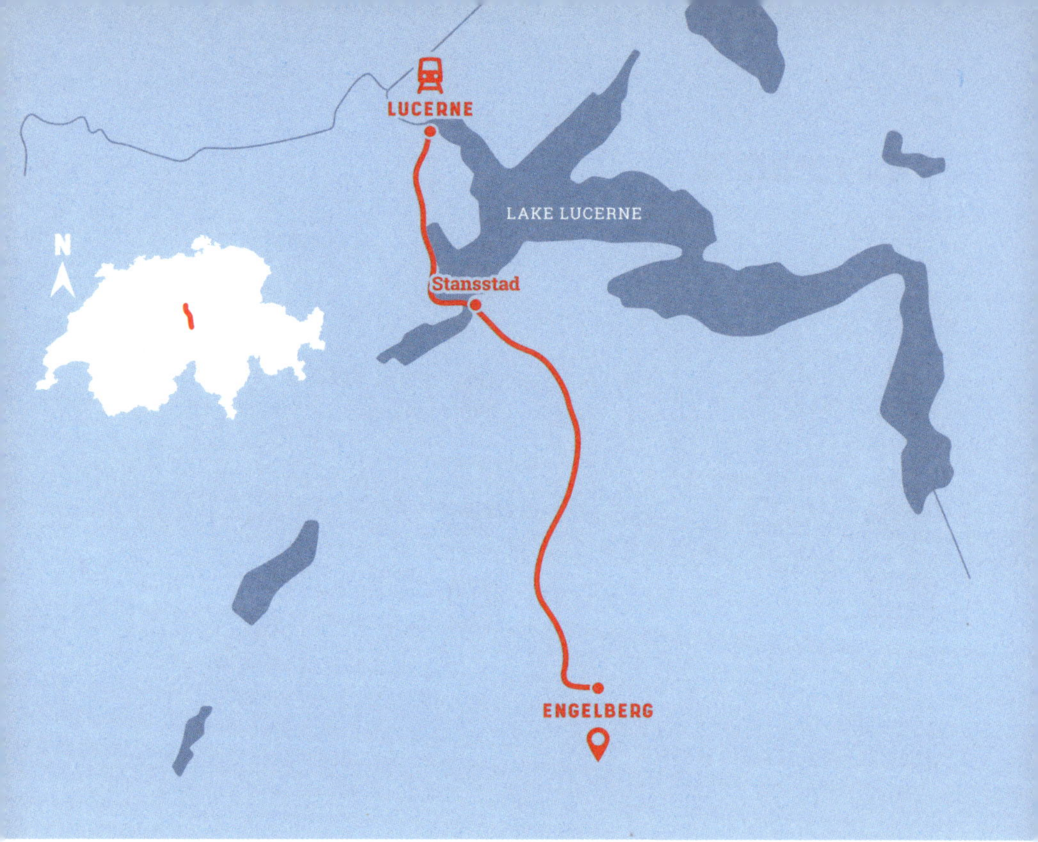

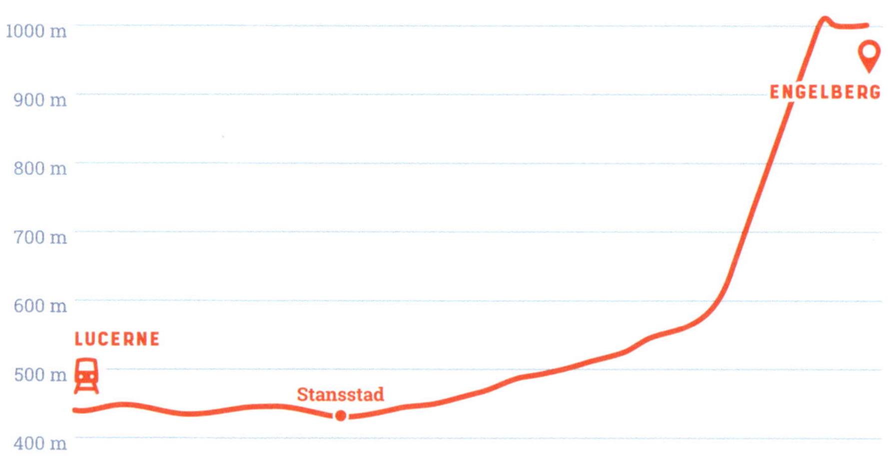

THE ROUTE

Ignore the Lucerne suburbs and wait for the drama of the lake opening up on the left-hand side, with the water sometimes so close it's practically lapping at the wheels of the train. With views on one side across the lake to Bürgenstock and on the other up to craggy Pilatus, it's great no matter which way you look.

After the bridge at Stansstad, the route is still flat but much greener, with the lake now replaced by fields and gardens. Past the towering mass of Stanserhorn, one of my favourite mountain excursions, things become more bucolic, with smaller towns and larger hills as the train heads up Engelberger Aa valley. After Wolfenschiessen, the landscape gets ever more rugged and rustic as the valley narrows.

Then the steady climb to Engelberg at 999m starts in earnest, using a rack railway for this last third of the journey, although the steepest section has been replaced by a tunnel. You're plunged into blackness only to emerge surrounded on three sides by mountains with the jagged skyline towering above you. Final destination: Engelberg, with its beautiful 12th-century monastery and the famous peak of Titlis as a backdrop.

THE HISTORY

Engelberg station in the winter of 1967.

Constructed by the Stansstad-Engelberg Railway, the metre-gauge line opened on 5 October 1898 and was electrified from the start, meaning that it was Switzerland's longest electric railway at that time. But as you might have noticed from the company name, the line ended at Stansstad, with the link to Lucerne by boat across the lake. The final section of the ascent to Engelberg was a steep rack railway, with a maximum gradient of 24.6% and carriages had to be pushed up by the locomotive. These facts all hampered the line's success and the railway company fell into financial difficulty in the 1950s.

It was rescued by the Nidwalden savings bank, and then relaunched as the Lucerne-Stans-Engelberg Railway (LSE) in 1964. A new bridge was built from Stansstad to Hergiswil so that the line could finally reach Lucerne, while longer, faster trains reduced travel times and increased capacity. The last improvement came in 2010, with the opening of the 4km-long Engelberg Tunnel, which cut the gradient to 10.5% and shaved about 15 minutes off the journey. In 2005, the LSE merged with the Brünig Railway to form the Zentralbahn, an independent subsidiary of SBB that also operates the Luzern–Interlaken Express.

TRIP TIPS

During the day, one carriage of the train is a Globi coach, named after the blue parrot that features in the popular Swiss children's books. It's a great spot for kids to enjoy the trip, with puzzles to solve along the way.

Get out at Stans for the unique trip to the top of Stanserhorn. First comes the historic funicular, dating back to 1893 with the original wooden carriages, then the very modern double-decker CabriO cable car. The open-air top deck has unforgettable views, complete with wind in your hair.

If you want to go even higher above Engelberg, then take the cable car to Titlis. It's actually two cable cars, the last one being the Rotair, which rotates as it rises giving everyone 360° views. The top station is at 3028m, just below the summit.

SOUTHERN SWITZERLAND

20 CENTOVALLI RAILWAY

Half Swiss, half Italian and a completely wonderful ride through the hills between Locarno and Domodossola.

Its name translates as 'a hundred valleys' but Centovalli is actually mainly used on the Swiss side. The Italians refer to this bi-national railway as the Vigezzina, after the Vigezzo valley, through which the railway runs to reach Domodossola. This is a remote corner of both Switzerland and Italy: the first road through here connecting the two countries only opened in 1907. And that's what makes this train trip so special: a chance to see unspoilt countryside outside the window.

From the beginning, this narrow-gauge railway was a joint project organised by the Swiss and Italians. And it remains a common endeavour, united by speaking the same language and both sides benefitting from this vital artery. The two operating companies are the Italian SSIF (short for Società Subalpina di Imprese Ferroviarie) and, in Switzerland, the Ferrovie Autolinee Regionali Ticinesi, shortened to FART. Every train is emblazoned with that rather unfortunate four-letter acronym.

FAST FACTS

START
Locarno

END
Domodossola

DISTANCE
52km

TIME NEEDED
1h 49min

HEIGHT DIFFERENCE
638m

WHERE TO SIT
On the left in Switzerland, right in Italy

PASSES
GA & Swiss Travel Pass: free; Half Fare card: 50% discount

NEARBY LINES
Geneva–Brig 5
Monte Generoso 25
Gotthard Railway 26

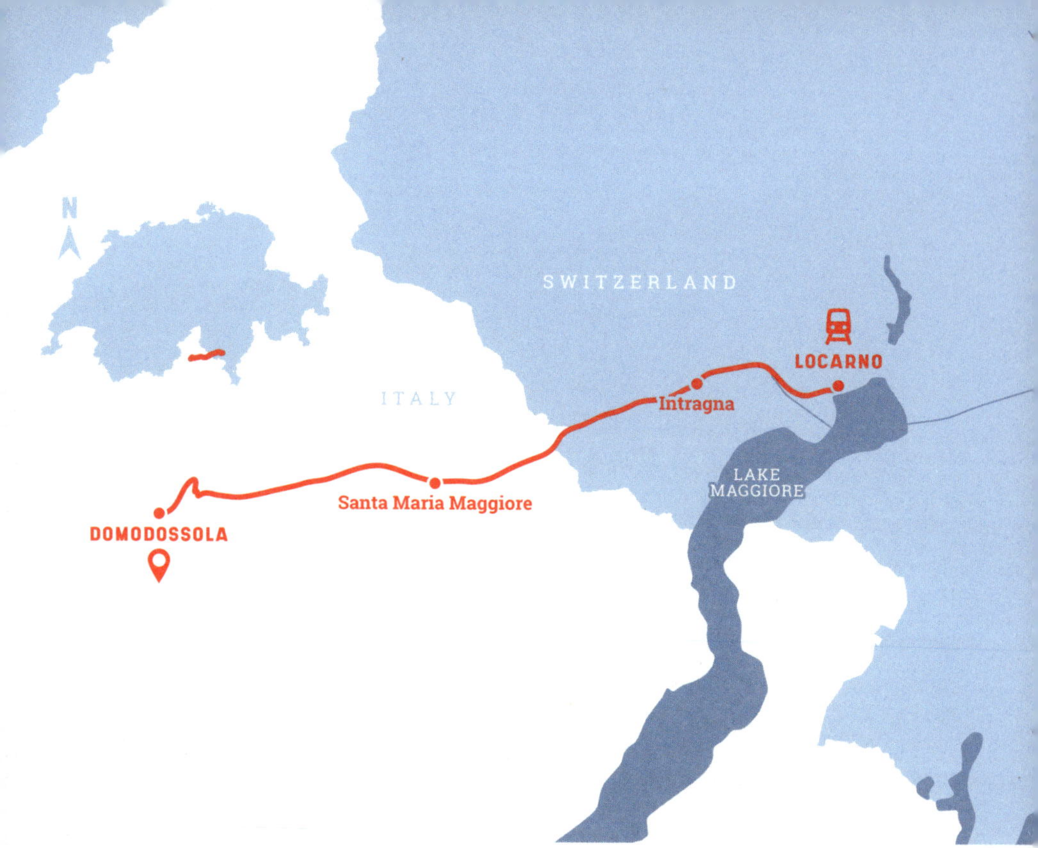

N
SWITZERLAND
ITALY
LOCARNO
Intragna
Santa Maria Maggiore
DOMODOSSOLA
LAKE
MAGGIORE

800 m
700 m
600 m
500 m
400 m
300 m
200 m
Santa Maria Maggiore
LOCARNO
Intragna
DOMODOSSOLA

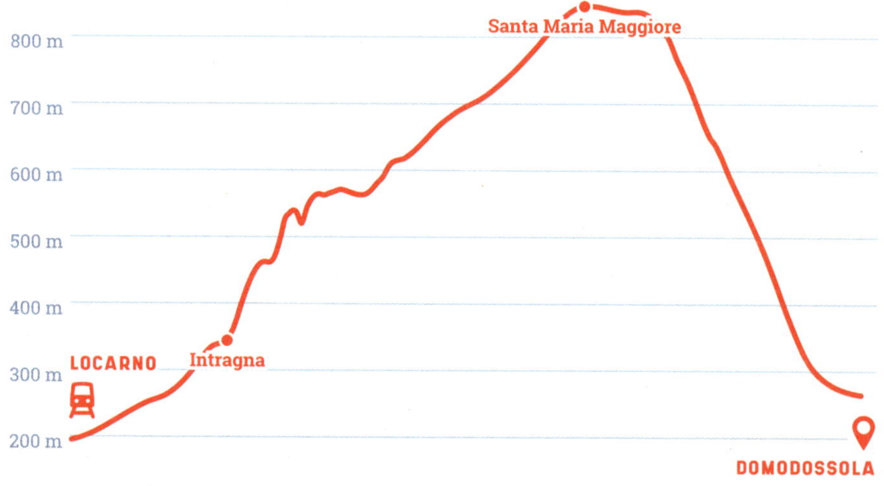

THE ROUTE

It all starts underground, so for the first five minutes you see nothing but darkness, but then you emerge into the bright light at Ponte Brolla, where the Maggia and Melezza rivers meet. The railway follows the latter, climbing up along the right-hand side of the valley, meaning the views of vineyards and villages are on the left.

Just before Intragna, get ready for an iconic shot on the left: the village perched on a hill with the steel rail bridge (and modern road bridge) in the foreground. From then on, the valley gets deeper and steeper, with heavily wooded slopes and cascading waterfalls: it all feels rather wild and barely inhabited. Shortly before the border station of Camedo comes the Ruinacci Viaduct, another impressive steel bridge – this one stands 55 metres above the rocky river below.

On the Italian side, the ride isn't as smooth so get ready to be jiggled and jostled on the long climb up to Santa Maria Maggiore, the highest point of the line at 831m. Switch here to sit on the right to see the ever-more jagged skyline and the village of Coimo clinging to the slopes opposite. There's a final grand view of the wide valley and snowy Alps on the horizon, and you descend into Domodossola.

THE HISTORY

Photo from the 1930s of the Isorno bridge in Ticino.

In 1898 the mayor of Locarno, Francesco Balli, turned vague ideas into concrete plans by applying to the Federal Council for a concession to build a line through the Centovalli to Italy. The opening of the Simplon Tunnel in 1906 increased the impetus for a direct connection between Domodossola and the Gotthard line. Both countries were keen to kickstart the development of this isolated region, so an Italian–Swiss committee was founded and financing secured from the Franco-American Bank in Paris. Construction began in 1912 under the engineer Giacomo Sutter. But events overwhelmed the project: the bank went bankrupt and the world went to war.

Work did not resume until 1921 and even then, the technical challenges of building a railway line through the wild landscape remained. Crossing the deep valleys and steep mountainsides required 83 viaducts and 31 tunnels to be constructed, and the line was finally inaugurated on 25 November 1923. At that time, it ended in Ponte Brolla but was eventually extended to Locarno four years later, with the trains terminating in the square in front of the station. The modern underground section opened in December 1990. One interesting side note: international traffic continued along the Centovalli line for the early part of the Second World War, only ending when Italy collapsed in September 1943.

TRIP TIPS

The train offers free wifi on board, which is useful if you don't have roaming (remember this is a cross-border service); scan the QR code that's posted in the carriages for an online guide to the route and all the stations.

The hourly service means you can get off to explore villages along the way, and re-board a later train. The narrow alleys of Intragna are overshadowed by the tallest bell tower in Ticino, while the Italian village of Re is famous for its pilgrimage church of Madonna del Sangue.

Even though half the line is in Italy, the whole journey is covered by Swiss travel passes (GA, Half Fare card and Swiss Travel Pass). This is mainly because it's the easiest way to travel between Ticino and Suisse Romande or the Bernese Oberland, via the line through the Simplon Tunnel to Brig.

21 GLACIER EXPRESS

From St Moritz to Zermatt, this is an extravaganza of scenery with glaciers, gorges, mountains and meadows.

Sitting surrounded by glass on three sides, literally watching the world go by and relaxing for a whole day. If that sounds like heaven on wheels, then you'll love this train ride. With meals served at your seat and great scenery as a moving backdrop, the Glacier Express is truly a trip to relish. It's not fast (the express refers to the lack of stops) and it's long (over eight hours) but with 291 bridges, 91 tunnels and two big altitude changes, it's the perfect way to see Switzerland. And it runs in both summer and winter.

This is the longest train trip possible in Switzerland without changing trains – but only if you're on the official Glacier Express. You can take regular trains along the same route but then you must change trains at various points. This chapter is divided into four sections, each of which can be travelled on its own or together they make up the entire Glacier Express journey. You don't have to travel the whole route but if you have the time, then do it in one go.

FAST FACTS

START
St Moritz

END
Zermatt

DISTANCE
291km

TIME NEEDED
8h 19min

HEIGHT DIFFERENCE
1464m

WHERE TO SIT
Both sides

PASSES
GA & Swiss Travel Pass: free;
Half Fare card: 50% discount

NEARBY LINES
Geneva–Brig 5
Furka Steam Railway 23
Bernina Express 28

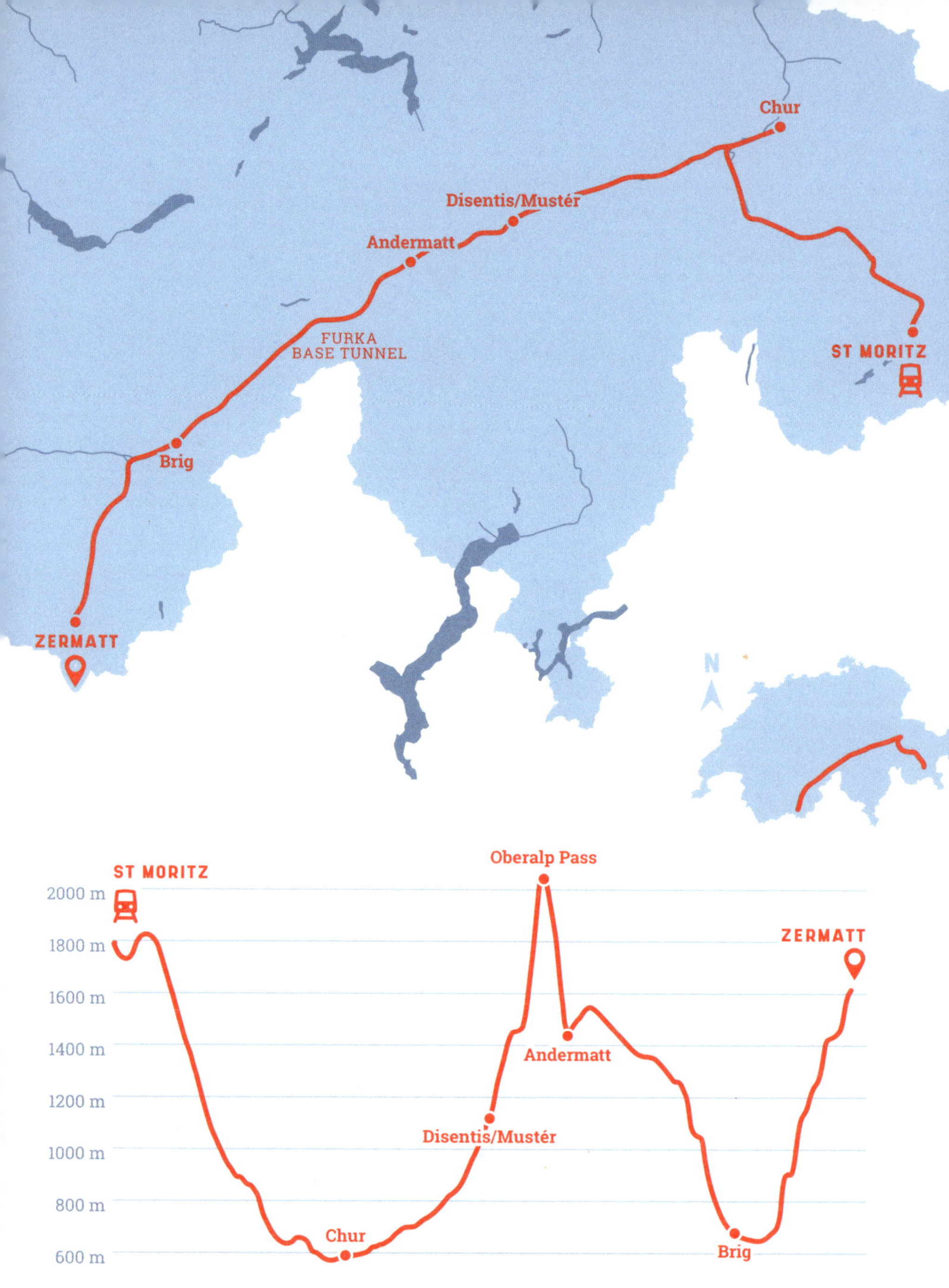
Chur
Disentis/Mustér
Andermatt
FURKA
BASE TUNNEL
ST MORITZ
Brig
ZERMATT
N
ST MORITZ
2000 m
1800 m
1600 m
1400 m
1200 m
1000 m
800 m
600 m
Oberalp Pass
ZERMATT
Andermatt
Disentis/Mustér
Chur
Brig

TRIP TIPS

Seat reservations are mandatory for all passengers on the Glacier Express and can be booked online. The posh Excellence Class has a hefty extra fee on top of the First Class ticket, but includes a five-course meal with wine and guaranteed window seats. In First and Second Class, meals are served at your seat but cost extra.

Taking the Glacier Express means no changing trains and enjoying carriages with big picture windows. If it's booked out, or you fancy riding like a local, catch a regular service: no reservation is required and you'll need to bring your own food and drink.

Going westwards (as described here) isn't so different from the reverse direction. Both have the same scenic highlights, with westwards benefitting from the gradual ascent to Zermatt and eastwards slightly better for the Landwasser Viaduct (pictured below).

ALBULA LINE

A crowd-pleaser since it opened in 1903, this spectacular line is still wowing passengers over a century later. Wonderful mountain scenery combined with incredible engineering: what more could you want?

THE ROUTE

Travelling from St Moritz, it isn't long before you leave the beautiful Engadin Valley and are plunged into the darkness of the Albula Tunnel, a centrepiece of the line. After that the magic really begins, with the incredible route down to Bergün. The railway uses long bridges and spiral tunnels to crisscross the river and lose height, curling and looping round on itself. And all the while, surrounded by mountains on both sides.

The undoubted highlight is one of Switzerland's most famous bridges: the Landwasser Viaduct. At 65m high, 122m long and supported by five towering arches, it almost defies belief that this was built. Travelling in this direction is possibly not as dramatic as going southwards (for that, read about the Bernina Express , p. 176), but it's still a thrill to emerge from a tunnel straight onto the bridge that starts flush with the cliff face. Sit at the front on the left for the full effect.

From then on, it's downhill all the way but that's no easy task as the train must master the narrow Albula Valley with its steep sides and rushing river. Here too are elaborate constructions, such as the 11-arch Solis Viaduct: it's the highest bridge of the line, standing 89m above the river below. After Thusis, the landscape relaxes a little, running alongside the Rhine to Chur.

THE HISTORY

The Albula Line features in both the Bernina Express (p. 176) and the Glacier Express but it's the same line with the same history.

Before the Albula Line was built, it was a hard slog to reach the Engadin. A 14-hour coach ride from St Moritz to Chur wasn't exactly conducive to comfortable travel, let alone transporting goods. Once the railway had reached Thusis in 1896, construction began on the line through the mountains just two years later. But it wasn't easy. Not only was the topography challenging but simply getting the materials to the sites was daunting, even though locally quarried limestone was used to build the viaducts. Every section was meticulously planned and built to a precise timetable.

Excavating the Albula Tunnel was particularly strenuous but the final breakthrough came in 1902, precipitating a fast completion of the line, which finally opened to great acclaim on 1 July 1903 (although St Moritz wasn't connected until a year later). It's stayed much the same since then, apart from electrification in 1919 and the new 5.9km-long Albula Tunnel II that opened in 2024. By the way, the Albula Line holds the world record for the longest passenger train – in 2022, Rhaetian Railway ran a train with 100 carriages, reaching a total length of 1.9km.

Building the Solis Viaduct in 1900 wasn't for the faint-hearted or anyone with vertigo.

CHUR ↔ ANDERMATT

This section along the Surselva Line is one of the most scenic rides in the whole country, so get ready for some picture-perfect moments, such as the Rhine Gorge – Switzerland's mini Grand Canyon.

THE ROUTE

Not long after Chur comes the natural wonder of the Rhine Gorge. In a vast landslide 10,000 years ago, over 10 billion cubic metres of rock cascaded into the valley, only for the river to slowly carve its way through. This landscape of white cliffs and weird shapes isn't quite as big as the Grand Canyon (only 13km long and 400m deep) but it looks great from the train. Sit on the right for the best views.

After that drama comes the gentler landscape of green fields and small villages. Many have bilingual German-Romansh names, as does the next main stop, Disentis/Mustér, with its grandiose Baroque monastery. If you're travelling on regular trains, this is where the Rhaetian Railway ends, so you must switch to the Matterhorn Gotthard Railway.

It's a long steady climb up to the Oberalp Pass (2033m, and the highest point of the whole Glacier Express), and a memorable one as the countryside gets wilder and the trees sparser. One oddity is the highest lighthouse in the world, originally from the Rhine delta but now beside a lake near the source of the river. Then on downhill through the high open valley surrounded by peaks, before the steep descent into Andermatt. The railway switchbacks its way down, intertwined with a serpentine road, both heading for the mountain resort.

THE HISTORY

Celebrations to mark the opening of Disentis/Mustér station on 1 August 1912.

It's only 59km from Chur to Disentis/Mustér but building the line wasn't as easy as that sounds. Not because of the altitude gain of 560m but because the topography of the area presented unique challenges. The first section to Reichenau-Tamins opened in 1896 but from there westwards various options were drawn up involving an array of viaducts and tunnels. In the end the most direct route through the Rhine Gorge was selected and in 1898 the Rhaetian Railway started planning the Surselva Line – exactly at the same time the company was building the Albula Line.

The chosen route was shorter but problematic, thanks to the fragile rock and constant risk of flooding, but even so the line opened as far as Ilanz in 1903, after only three years' work. The extension to Disentis/Mustér was delayed but finally finished in 1912. Building in the other direction, from Andermatt up and over the Oberalp Pass, took longer, mainly because the Brig-Furka-Disentis company went bankrupt. Its successor, the Furka-Oberalp Railway, completed the missing link in July 1926 with the help of federal funding.

ANDERMATT ↔ BRIG

A gentle descent from the high Alpine meadows of the Reuss Valley down through the rolling foothills to the broad swathe of the Rhone Valley and the trio of towers crowning the Stockalper Castle in Brig.

THE ROUTE

If you stop off in Andermatt, one little diversion is the short but dramatic train ride through the narrow Schöllenen Gorge to Göschenen (where the north-south trains to Ticino stop). I like to take this train one way, then hike back past the infamous Devil's Bridge. Or you could stay overnight and continue on the Glacier Express the next day.

The journey westwards continues through the almost-empty landscape to the Furka Base Tunnel, 15.4km long and built under the Furka Pass to make the line usable all year round. In summer, you can still enjoy the scenery along the original line from Realp by taking the Furka Steam Railway (see p. 146). Mainline trains, including the Glacier Express, always go via the tunnel, emerging into the clear air of serene Goms Valley.

From Oberwald up at 1366m, it's steadily downhill, sometimes past steeply wooded slopes, sometimes through calmer pastures. It's gently scenic rather than dramatic, with pretty villages dotted among the hills and glimpses of higher peaks. The line winds its way down, often needing cogs to help with the descent, all the while following the River Rhone, its water murky with sediment. A final spiral tunnel, a last narrow gorge and the train reaches Brig.

THE HISTORY

In 1910 the Brig-Furka-Disentis railway (BFD) was founded, mainly funded by French investors who had great influence over the planning. Construction began in the summer of 1911 and the first section between Brig and Gletsch was opened to great fanfare in June 1914. It all looked good for extending the line eastwards. Then came the First World War. French money dried up and the Italian rail workers went home. Although the first breakthrough in the original Furka Tunnel was achieved in 1915, all work was abandoned a year later. In 1923 the BFD was declared bankrupt.

A rail connection from Valais to Graubünden was too important to fail, so a new company was founded in 1925, with financial backing of the Swiss government. The Furka-Oberalp Railway re-started construction on the line immediately and on 4 July 1926 the first trains ran from Brig to Disentis. The line was electrified in 1941–42 but it could not be used year-round until 1982, when the 15.4km-long Furka Base Tunnel opened. At that time, it was the longest metre-gauge tunnel in the world. Today, the line is operated by the Matterhorn Gotthard Railway.

A 1959 poster by Hugo Schol with the old route before the Base Tunnel opened.

BRIG ↔ ZERMATT

This is a tale of two valleys: the flat expanse of the Rhone and the steep-sided walls of the Matter Vispa. And the undoubted highlight is the first glimpse of that iconic peak, the Matterhorn.

THE ROUTE

After its languid meanderings through the high Alpine valleys, the train positively races along the flat stretch of land beside the milky green Rhone. Terraced vineyards cling to the south-facing slopes, while rail, road and river all run alongside each other until Visp, where the main line comes in from the north.

Then it's southwards, into the heart of the Valais Alps so it's no surprise that a rack railway is needed. At first the steep valley is best seen from the left, with a grandstand view of sheer gorges and the onion-domed church at St Niklaus. But the higher you go, the better the views on the right as rocky mountains start to dominate the landscape. The carriages jiggle and jolt each time a section of rack railway is needed to master the gradient.

After Herbriggen, a big wide curve gives a perfect panorama on the right of the mighty Weisshorn and its glacier. Waterfalls cascade down the rocks, sadly a sign of the glaciers melting, and the snowy peaks become larger and larger. One final rack section for the last climb, and 90 minutes after leaving Brig (and over eight hours after leaving St Moritz) the train pulls into Zermatt, 1605m up. If you're lucky, you'll get a quick peek of the Matterhorn just before the station. Or simply walk into the centre of the village for the perfect photo spot.

THE HISTORY

Given the popularity of Zermatt, it seems obvious that it would have a train connection to the rest of Switzerland. But replacing the old mule track up the valley wasn't that easy for the Visp Zermatt Railway company, which started construction in 1888. Resistance from locals made buying the land along the route a long and difficult process, while no road meant that all building materials had to be transported by rail as each section was completed. There was also the risk of landslides and the challenge of long winters, but the line finally reached Zermatt in July 1891.

It was an immediate success and passenger numbers exploded. But there was one problem: the connection between Visp and Brig. The line to Zermatt has a metre gauge but the mainline along the Rhone Valley is standard gauge, so passengers had to change trains. Eventually a new metre-gauge railway was built from Visp to Brig, meaning that the inaugural Glacier Express service could leave Zermatt for St Moritz on 25 June 1930. Trains to Zermatt were not year-round until 1933, when the construction of avalanche galleries made a continuous winter service possible.

Poster from 1895 by F. Hugo d'Alési showing the then-new line to Zermatt.

22 MONT-BLANC EXPRESS

Scenic line through the mountains that straddle the Swiss–French border, linking Martigny with Chamonix-Mont-Blanc.

You're sitting in your window seat (on the left, as I recommend here) and enjoying the views high up above Martigny. The staggeringly deep Trient Valley, the acres of wild woods, the villages perched precariously on cliff tops – it's all wonderful. And then you cross the border into France, and have to change trains. For a line that's marketed as one scenic train ride, it's unbelievably silly to make passengers change to an identical train purely because they have crossed the border.

But that's the only downside of this beautiful trip through the Alps. To compensate for the two countries and two train companies being unable to provide a seamless service, the whole journey is a delight from start to finish. You start in the wide Rhone Valley, climb up through thick forests to the border, then descend past rocky pinnacles and finish at the foot of Mont Blanc.

FAST FACTS

START
Martigny

END
Chamonix-Mont-Blanc

DISTANCE
38km

TIME NEEDED
1h 27min

HEIGHT DIFFERENCE
795m

WHERE TO SIT
On the left towards Chamonix

PASSES
In Switzerland, GA & Swiss Travel Pass: free; Half Fare card: 50% discount

NEARBY LINES
Geneva–Brig 5
The Lötschberger 17
St-Bernard Express 27

TMR

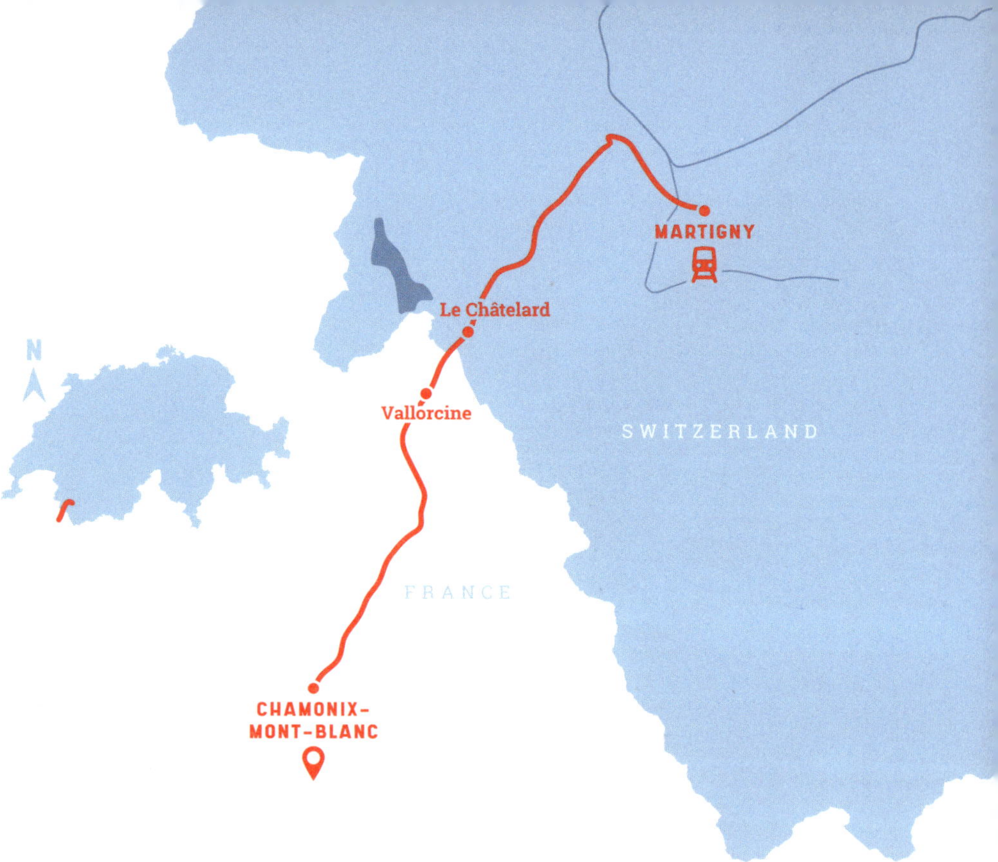

N
MARTIGNY
Le Châtelard
Vallorcine
SWITZERLAND
FRANCE
CHAMONIX-
MONT-BLANC

1400 m
1200 m
1000 m
800 m
600 m
400 m
Vallorcine
Le Châtelard
CHAMONIX-MONT-BLANC
MARTIGNY

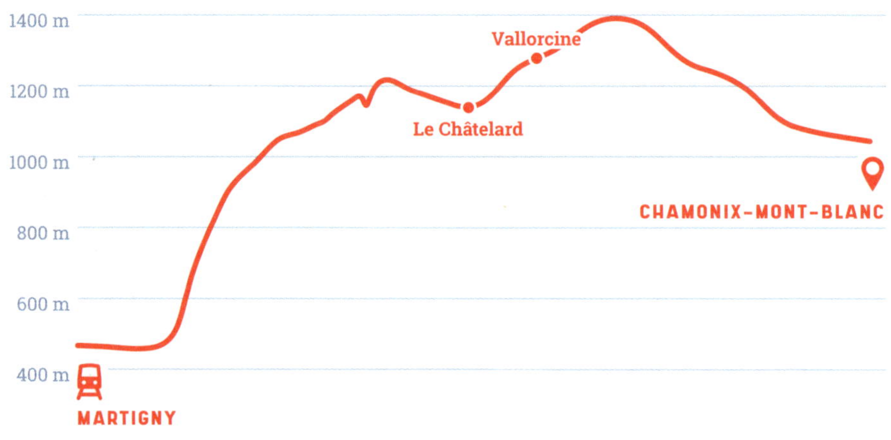

THE ROUTE

After racing along the flat valley from Martigny, the steep climb begins after the Trient Gorge, helped by a section of rack railway with a 20% gradient. Here the views are on the right, with a great near-aerial perspective of the elbow bend of the River Rhone. After that, it pays to sit on the left.

The train clings to the top of the deep valley of the River Trient, with tiny villages like Le Trétien huddled on vertiginous cliffs and endless trees in every direction. At Finhaut, there's a perfect view on the left as the first big mountains appear on the horizon. After the border at Le Châtelard, you're in France and that means an annoying change of trains at Vallorcine.

And the scenery changes too, for the better as it gets even more dramatic. Nothing quite prepares you for the first clear view of a jagged skyline of peaks and ever-white Mont Blanc. It's truly magnificent. The long, slow descent from Argentière is filled with such a grand spectacle of mountain scenery (at least if you sit on the left) that you want every minute to last twice as long.

THE HISTORY

Clearing the snow between Martigny and Le Châtelard in 1976.

It all began in 1901. In that year, the Swiss government granted a concession for a narrow-gauge line between Martigny and Le Châtelard via Finhaut; there had been other plans for a railway via the nearby Col de la Forclaz. In the same year on the French side, the Paris-Lyon-Méditerranée Railway reached Chamonix with its line from St Gervais. Work began on connecting the two sides in 1902, with both countries working separately but towards a common goal. The whole line was designed to be electrified from the start, and, unusually for Switzerland, partly powered by a separate third rail next to the tracks rather than only overhead cables.

The Swiss section to Le Châtelard was inaugurated on 20 August 1906 while the French completed their line as far as Argentière that same summer. Finally, the missing link of 9.6km between the two separate sections was opened on 1 July 1908. Winter services began in 1935 with the building of avalanche galleries. Since 2001 the Swiss side has been operated by TMR (Transports de Martigny et Régions), along with the neighbouring St-Bernard Express. The French side has been run since 1938 by the national rail company, SNCF.

TRIP TIPS

The journey to the border station at Le Châtelard-Frontière is covered by Swiss travel passes (GA, Half Fare card and Swiss Travel Pass). To continue into France, you must get a ticket and there is no discount for having a Swiss travel pass. You can usually buy tickets on the train before you cross the border.

One highlight is the Trient Gorge: get off at Vernayaz and the entrance to the gorge is next to the station. The 200m-deep canyon was carved by the River Trient and can be explored via wooden boardwalks attached to the sheer rocks. Remember to look up to see the Pont de Gueuroz, one of the highest bridges in Europe.

In Chamonix, stay long enough to take the mountain train (pictured below) up to Montenvers beside the Mer de Glace. The once-mighty glacier is still there (just) but the ride up in the little red train is definitely worth doing. Sit on the left going uphill for the best views.

23 FURKA STEAM RAILWAY

Nostalgic train ride with historic engines along the old mountain route that is a delightful trip into the past.

Every summer, from late June to late September, the huffing and puffing of a massive steam engine can be heard echoing through the Alpine landscape of southern Switzerland. It threads its way through the thick forests, rumbles across old bridges and climbs up (and down) hills. This is the Furka Steam Railway, one of the best heritage lines in Switzerland; both for the scenic route and the nostalgic feel.

But this beautiful train ride doesn't come without its challenges. It takes time to reach the start/end points high up in the mountains and it's essential to plan ahead. The steam trains only run twice a day, Thursday to Sunday, and easily sell out. Booking online in advance means taking a chance with the weather but it's worth the risk. This is one of Switzerland's most memorable railways, all the more so because it almost disappeared and is now run largely by volunteers.

FAST FACTS

START
Realp

DISTANCE
17.8km

HEIGHT DIFFERENCE
797m

PASSES
GA & Half Fare card: variable discounts; Swiss Travel Pass: not valid

END
Oberwald

TIME NEEDED
2h 15min

WHERE TO SIT
On the right towards Oberwald

NEARBY LINES
Geneva–Brig 5
Glacier Express 21
Gotthard Railway 26

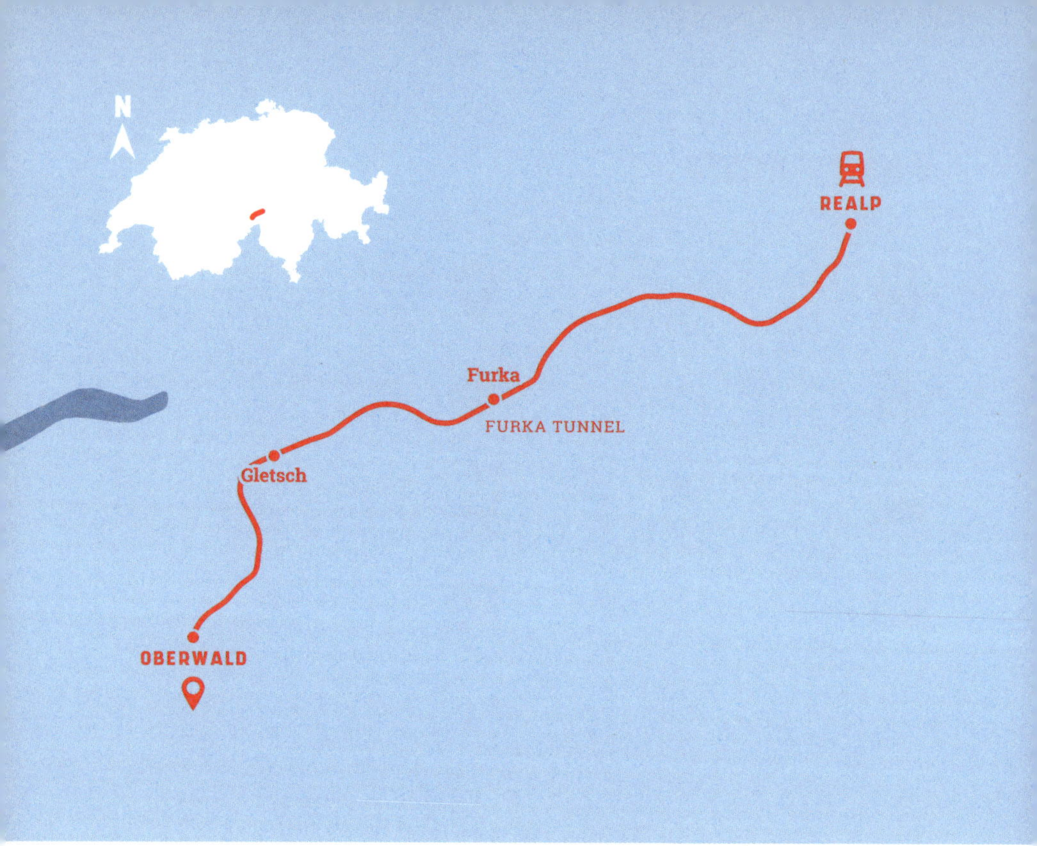

N

REALP

Furka

FURKA TUNNEL

Gletsch

OBERWALD

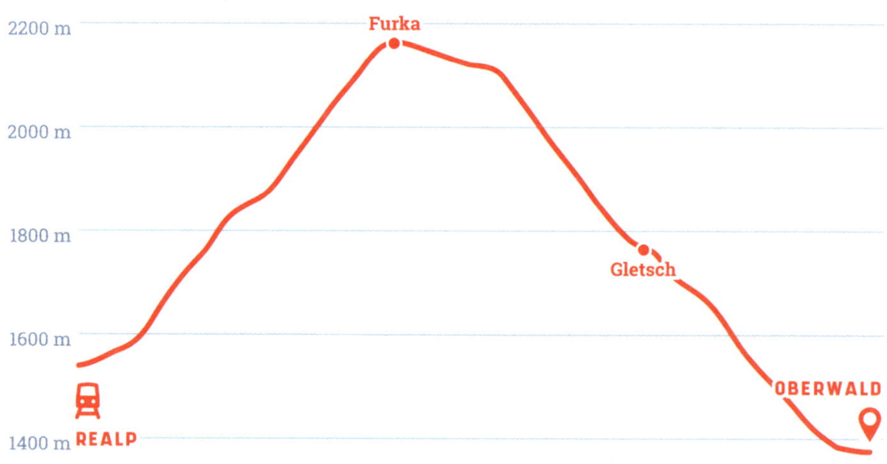

THE ROUTE

The Furka line is just under 18km but packs a lot into that distance, not least the departure. It's thrilling to watch a restored steam engine pull into Realp station, its brass fittings gleaming in the sun, and then board the smart old carriages. Whistle blowing, steam billowing, you're off on a journey into the past.

As you chug through lush fields dotted with cows and slowly climb past tumbling brooks, watch out for the Steffenbach Bridge. This one is special as it folds up to be dismantled each autumn to protect it from avalanches. At the highest point (Furka, 2163m) there's a longer stop for tea (and toilets!) as it's where the up and down trains cross. Then on into the 1874m-long Furka Tunnel, so close the windows or you'll be splattered with black specks. Yes, real coal is used to make the steam.

Out of the tunnel and over into Valais. Sit on the right for perfect views of the Furka pass road (star of Goldfinger) zigzagging over the hills, and then the Rhone Glacier, or at least where it used to be. This railway once ran beside the ice but now it's only newly-exposed rock and fresh waterfalls, albeit very pretty ones. After Gletsch, it's steeply downhill to Oberwald and the end of the line.

THE HISTORY

A photo from 1926 when the Rhone glacier was still quite impressive.

The story of the Furka line is as convoluted as the route it takes through the mountains. In 1911 the Brig-Furka-Disentis Railway (BFD) began construction on the narrow-gauge cogwheel line. Within four years the first section from Brig to Gletsch was complete and the tunnel breakthrough had been achieved. But then the money ran out, construction stopped and in 1923 BFD was declared bankrupt. Thankfully the Furka-Oberalp-Bahn was set up and work resumed. In 1926 the Brig-Andermatt-Disentis route was officially declared open.

Once the line was electrified in 1942, some of the old steam trains were sent to Vietnam; others decommissioned completely. But the line still had to close for seven months a year thanks to the avalanche risk. The opening of the new Furka Base Tunnel in 1982 made year-round services possible but also meant the old mountain line fell into disrepair. It was rescued by volunteers and donations, and slowly restored, with three steam engines coming back from Vietnam to ride these rails again. The first section re-opened in 1992 and the final one from Gletsch to Oberwald on 12 August 2010. Trains could once again run along the original route between cantons Uri and Valais, along what is now the longest operated unelectrified line in Switzerland.

TRIP TIPS

Starting in Realp and going westwards is marginally better as a steam engine alone is enough for the whole trip. Travelling eastwards from Oberwald, the train also needs a diesel engine to help it master the long incline up to the Furka Tunnel.

Seat reservations are compulsory and you can book online to be sure of getting on board. It's often sold out, and then the small wooden seats in Second Class can feel rather cramped – First Class is worth the extra money for more comfort.

Holders of a GA or Half Fare card get a variable discount on all tickets. Children aged six to 16 travel free with a Junior Travelcard when accompanied by their parents.

24 GORNERGRAT

Mountains galore along this historic rack railway that almost puts all others in the shade with its incredible views.

At 3098m, Gornergrat has an impressive collection of superlatives: the highest open-air station and highest open-air rack railway in Europe, plus Switzerland's highest hotel, are all remarkable feats, though being Switzerland's first fully electrified mountain railway isn't shabby either. This short but spectacular ride has been thrilling guests from all around the world since it opened in 1898 and it's still one of the most scenic train trips around. It truly takes Swiss rock-and-ice scenery to another level.

Many people come up here from Zermatt for the perfect views of Switzerland's most iconic mountain, the Matterhorn. It can be seen along the whole route – but only if you sit on the right as you go up. However, there are 28 other peaks over 4000m on display, including the country's highest mountain, Dufourspitze, which clocks in at 4634m. Plus, there are the grand glaciers that slowly carve their way between all the jagged summits on either side.

FAST FACTS

START
Zermatt

END
Gornergrat

DISTANCE
9.3km

TIME NEEDED
38min

HEIGHT DIFFERENCE
1485m

WHERE TO SIT
On the right going uphill

PASSES
GA, Swiss Travel Pass & Half Fare card: 50% discount

NEARBY LINES
Geneva–Brig 

Glacier Express 21
Mont-Blanc Express 22

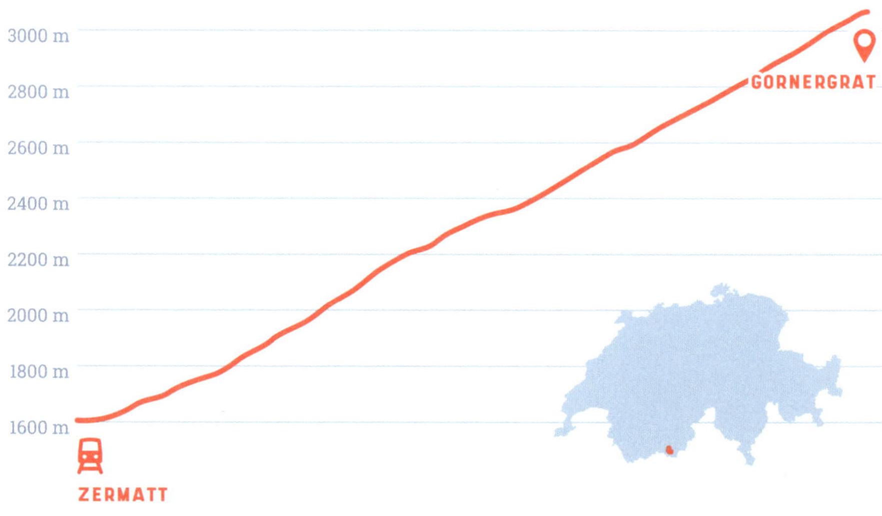
3000 m
2800 m
2600 m
2400 m
2200 m
2000 m
1800 m
1600 m
GORNERGRAT
ZERMATT

THE ROUTE

As the train pulls out of the valley station, you get your first glimpse of the Matterhorn behind all the chalets and hotels. The higher you climb, the clearer the view, until you pass the edge of the stone pine forest – then that singular triangular mountain is revealed in all its magnificent glory.

Tickets are valid for getting off and on along the way. So you can hop off at any stop, either to hike one section (see Trip tips overleaf) or simply to take photos before getting back on a later train. A great stop for that is Rotenboden, where it's a short walk down to Riffelsee for the famous Matterhorn reflection (when there's no wind).

Once at Gornergrat itself, be sure to walk up to the top viewpoint above the hotel. From there, the 360° panorama encompasses so many lofty peaks that the Matterhorn is just one summit among many. You feel like you're on top of the world, with glaciers at your feet and crisp, thin air in your lungs. The hotel terrace is the ideal spot for lunch in the sun before heading back down to Zermatt.

THE HISTORY

Poster showing the timetable for 1899, the second year of operations.

Gornergrat was a very popular spot long before the railway was even proposed, despite the four-hour hike to get there. It appeared in Baedeker's guidebooks and attracted visitors from far and wide, including one Mark Twain. In 1878 he wrote: 'Nowhere else is there such an exhibition of size and beauty as can be seen from the summit of the Gornergrat.' So it's perhaps no surprise that this became the site for the first electric rack railway in Switzerland, and the first train in Europe that travelled up over 3000m. It was a line designed purely as a tourist attraction.

There was stiff local opposition to the railway, with many fearing it would destroy the livelihoods of guides and porters. A second proposed line to the Matterhorn was turned down but the Swiss government gave the go-ahead to the Gornergrat railway and construction started in May 1896. Work could only take place in summer but just two summers later, on 20 August 1898, the first train clambered up to Gornergrat. This new attraction put Zermatt firmly on the tourist map, quashing fears of its negative effects. Winter services began in 1928 and the train still runs all year round.

TRIP TIPS

When you buy your tickets, add in priority boarding. That lets you jump the queue in Zermatt, so that you board the train first and can nab the seats on the right for the best views – ideal for peak periods when it can be really busy.

My favourite Gornergrat activity is to hike part of the way down from the top and catch the train again at Riffelberg. The descent takes about 90 minutes, with a height difference of 500m, and has picture-perfect views all the way, including at Riffelsee.

Or you could stay overnight in the 3100 Kulmhotel, with incomparable views, great food and comfy rooms. It's the highest hotel in the Swiss Alps, and once the last train has left, it's just the guests, the stars and the mountains. I loved it!

25 MONTE GENEROSO

From lakeside to mountain top, this is Ticino's highest railway line with views to match the altitude.

The bright orange train with the dark blue stripes is hard to miss but just in case you're in any doubt, look at the side of the carriages. There in giant capital letters are the words MONTE GENEROSO. Definitely the right train for going up one of the highest mountains in southern Ticino. And I rather like that they aren't fancy new carriages but older ones with windows that open. Fresh air and glass-free photos always make for a great train ride.

Taking the most southerly rack railway in Switzerland isn't only about the train ride. From the top station, you can hike higher up to the summit at 1704m for splendid views of the Alps, from Dufourspitze and the Matterhorn to the Gotthard massif. But there's also the national border with Italy, marked by small stone pillars. There aren't many places in Switzerland where you can take a train to a mountain top and stand with one foot in and one foot out of the country.

FAST FACTS

START
Capolago-Riva San Vitale

END
Monte Generoso

DISTANCE
9km

TIME NEEDED
40min

HEIGHT DIFFERENCE
1319m

WHERE TO SIT
Right then left

PASSES
GA, Swiss Travel Pass & Half Fare card: 50% discount

NEARBY LINES
Centovalli Railway 20
Glacier Express 21
Gotthard Railway 26

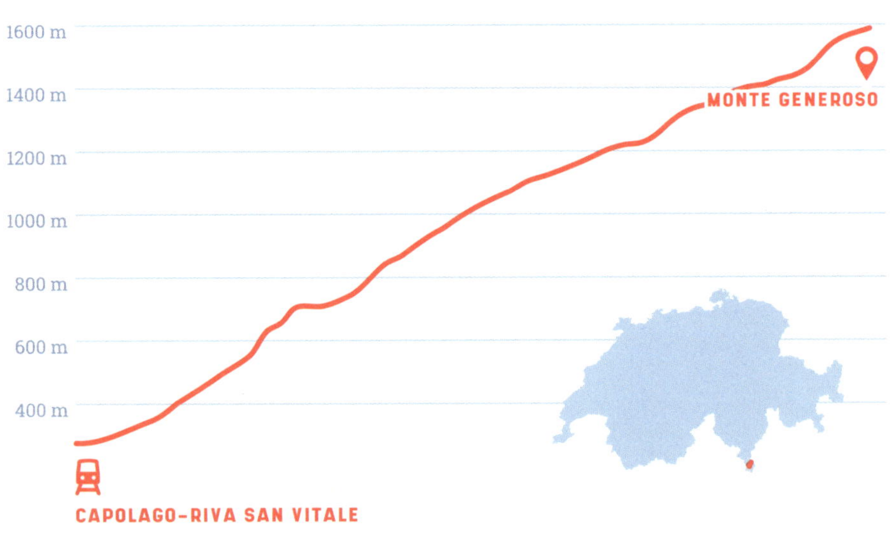
1600 m
1400 m
1200 m
1000 m
800 m
600 m
400 m
MONTE GENEROSO
CAPOLAGO-RIVA SAN VITALE

THE ROUTE

The route goes across the street, under the motorway and then steeply up the left-hand slope of the valley, hugging the mountain side so closely that the railway is almost part of the rock. Here the views are on the right, over the broad expanse of the plain with its motorway, train line and acres of solar panels.

On up through the trees, with views of Italy on the right: wooded hills, clusters of villages and the Po Valley beyond. This single-track railway has crossing points for the up and down trains to pass, such as at the aptly-named Bellavista, with its first glimpse of Lake Lugano. From here on, it's eyes left for the lake shots all the way up.

The only thing that will distract you from the views is the impressive building at the final stop (pictured below): the 'Fiore di pietra', or flower of stone, designed by local architect Mario Botta, who used to come up here as a child. It has grandstand views of the lake, or you can tackle the 15-minute hike to the summit for the full-on 360° panorama, usually complete with resident colony of chamois.

A poster from 1924, when a return ticket from Capolago cost 13 Swiss francs!

Mountain railways like these were built in the late 19th century primarily as tourist attractions but that doesn't mean they were always successful. In 1886, the Monte Generoso Railway won the concession for a narrow-gauge rack railway up the mountain, and ran its first steam train on 4 June 1890. But passenger numbers were too low and by 1904 the company had gone into liquidation. A new company was formed in 1909 but that one only lasted until 1914, when it, too, went bankrupt. It was resurrected two years later and this time survived until September 1939.

What the struggling rack railway needed was a guardian angel, and one with deep pockets. That came in the form of Gottlieb Duttweiler, founder of the Migros supermarket chain. He campaigned to save the line and in March 1941, Migros took over the Monte Generoso Railway – and still owns it today. The steam trains were replaced with diesel engines, and they in turn made way for electric ones in 1982. But one old steam engine is still in use, making special trips up to the summit on special occasions: it's the oldest steam locomotive still in operation in Switzerland.

TRIP TIPS

From Lugano you can reach Capolago in 15 minutes by train or you can take a boat. It's a leisurely 50-minute ride to the end of Lake Lugano where it's a short walk to the Monte Generoso train. Lovely, except sadly the boat only runs once a day, timed to connect with the first train up the mountain.

Free travel is possible, even in Switzerland. Go to Monte Generoso on your birthday and you'll get a free return ticket. And all year round, children up to 15 years old travel for free when accompanied by parents or grandparents. Babies and toddlers under five don't need a ticket.

As the border is only a few metres from the top station, your mobile phone will most likely connect to an Italian provider. You might get caught out if you don't have roaming outside Switzerland, so remember to switch off your mobile data (or use the wifi in the restaurant).

26 GOTTHARD RAILWAY

Three options, two tunnels and one monumental train ride through the mountains at the centre of Switzerland.

If there's one date that sums up Swiss railway history, it's 1 June 1882: the day the first passenger services rolled through the original Gotthard Tunnel. At that time, the tunnel was the longest in the world, but more importantly it connected north with south for the first time. This crucial artery through the heart of Switzerland transformed the national (and international) transport network but it's not only historic, it's also one of the best scenic train rides in the country.

That original tunnel has been superseded by the longer Base Tunnel, giving you a choice of three services for travelling to Ticino: the direct Intercity via the new tunnel, which is quicker but less scenic; the Gotthard Panorama Express, a summer-only tourist train along the old line; or the Treno Gottardo, a regular train from Basel or Zurich using the same panorama route, which will be the focus of this chapter.

FAST FACTS

START
Basel or Zurich

END
Locarno

DISTANCE
261km from Basel

TIME NEEDED
4h 21min from Basel

HEIGHT DIFFERENCE
946m

WHERE TO SIT
On the right going south

PASSES
GA & Swiss Travel Pass: free;
Half Fare card: 50% discount

NEARBY LINES
Centovalli Railway 20
Glacier Express 21
Voralpen-Express 29

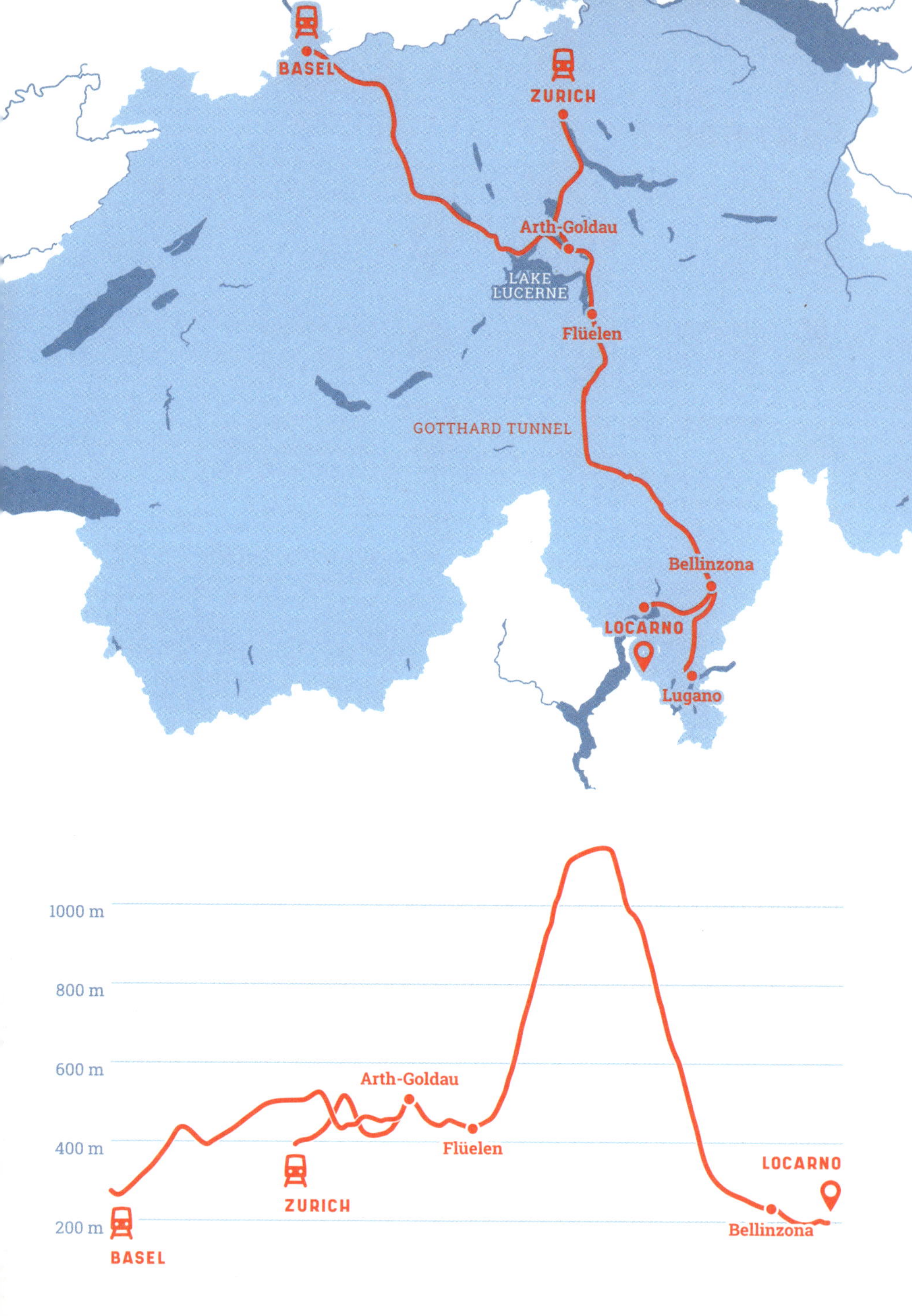

BASEL
ZURICH
Arth-Goldau
LAKE
LUCERNE
Flüelen
GOTTHARD TUNNEL
Bellinzona
LOCARNO
Lugano
1000 m
800 m
600 m
400 m
200 m
BASEL
ZURICH
Arth-Goldau
Flüelen
LOCARNO
Bellinzona

THE ROUTE

Starting in Zurich shaves an hour off the journey time, and gives you extra lake time to enjoy, whereas the trip from Basel meanders gently through the rolling landscape to Lucerne. The branches of the Treno Gottardo merge at Arth-Goldau, where the Panorama Express train also begins. Then on south past rugged hills and the glistening waters of Lake Lucerne on the right.

Lakes done, the mountains start in earnest at Flüelen, where the boat from Lucerne docks, along with the 19th-century engineering of spiral tunnels and vast viaducts. All the more impressive given that it's a main line, not narrow gauge or rack railway. At Wassen (pictured below), the church is seen from three different angles and heights as the train repeatedly curls up and around the village. The last station before the original tunnel is Göschenen, where you can change and take the little train to Andermatt for connections to east-west lines.

After the darkness, comes the light. Emerging from the tunnel at Airolo, the sky is often bluer, the sun brighter and the air warmer. Welcome to Ticino! The gradual descent through tree-clad hills needs more loops and tunnels until the castles of Bellinzona come into view. It's then a short hop down to Locarno on the shores of Lake Maggiore, the lowest point in Switzerland.

THE HISTORY

Building a railway through the Swiss Alps to connect Ticino with the rest of the country was a dream that took a while to realise. The Gotthard Railway Company, founded in 1871 and chaired by banker-politician Alfred Escher, was responsible for building both the line and the 15km tunnel. Louis Favre of Geneva was the chief engineer, and a new-fangled invention, dynamite, was used for blasting the rock at 1151m above sea level. Technical difficulties, poor ventilation, workers' strikes and Favre's death all caused delays but the tunnel breakthrough came on 29 February 1880. The full inauguration came two years later and the tunnel was hailed as a marvel of modern engineering.

What we today enjoy as a panoramic train trip eventually became too slow for the high level of traffic. It wasn't so much the tunnel itself but the cumbersome journey up and down to reach it, so a new tunnel – deeper, flatter, longer – was planned then approved by a national referendum. Construction took 17 years and cost over 12 billion Swiss francs, with the twin-tube tunnel finally opening on 1 June 2016; passenger services followed six months later. The Swiss had regained the title of the longest rail tunnel in the world (the Base Tunnel is 57.1km), and drastically cut travel times between north and south.

This 1927 poster from Swiss Federal Railways shows the timetable between Basel and Milan.

TRIP TIPS

It's First Class carriages only on the Gotthard Panorama Express and seat reservations are obligatory, even if you have a GA or Swiss Travel Pass. It runs from April to October and the whole route officially includes the boat ride between Lucerne and Flüelen, although you can just take the train.

The Treno Gottardo, operated by Südostbahn, runs every hour, with alternating departures from Basel or Zurich and stops frequently so you can get off and explore. Discover delightful towns like Altdorf, where the William Tell apple-shooting drama took place, or Bellinzona, the Ticinese capital dominated by three medieval castles.

Using the Gotthard Base Tunnel route is much quicker, with fewer stops and a faster flatter tunnel. It's also the easiest way to reach Lugano (and the Italian border at Chiasso) via a second new tunnel, the Ceneri Base Tunnel, which opened south of Bellinzona in 2020.

27 ST–BERNARD EXPRESS

A popular local line, especially for outdoor enthusiasts, that connects villages in two pretty valleys in Valais.

Welcome aboard the Y train, a short line that heads south from Martigny then splits in two, with each branch going up a different valley. It's a gently scenic ride with typically Swiss countryside of rolling hills and glimpses of distant mountains. Some might also think of it as the 'why' train: why build a railway that goes to two small villages then stops? It was originally planned to carry on over the Great St Bernard Pass but that never happened. Today its gentle appeal is more popular with hikers/skiers than tourists. Plus, it's far less busy than the nearby Mont-Blanc Express.

The left-hand branch of the Y serves as the main line, with direct trains going from Martigny to Le Châble, where you can catch a cable car up to the mountain resort of Verbier. Rather ironically, the older branch to Orsières is now the one without a direct service: you must change in Sembrancher to a connecting train for the short ride to the end of the line. In summer you can switch to a bus for the steep road up to the Great St Bernard pass and hospice.

FAST FACTS

START
Martigny

DISTANCE
25km

HEIGHT DIFFERENCE
434m

PASSES
GA & Swiss Travel Pass: free; Half Fare card: 50% discount

END
Orsières/Le Châble

TIME NEEDED
27min

WHERE TO SIT
On the right

NEARBY LINES
Geneva–Brig 5
The Lötschberger 17
Mont-Blanc Express 22

RegionAlps

THE ROUTE

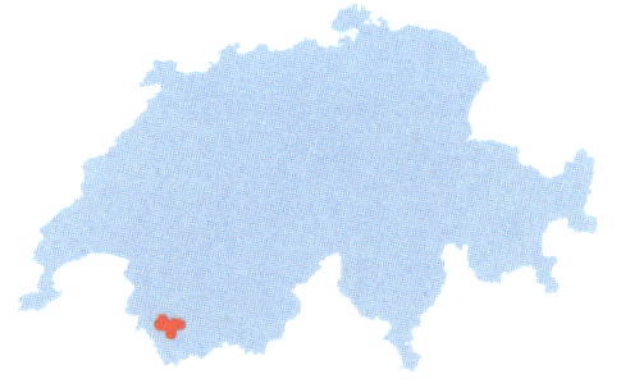

As the train pulls out of Martigny station, it feels instinctively like you're going in the wrong direction, up the Rhone Valley. Then the line makes a giant loop round behind the town before slowly climbing up through the vineyards clinging to the slopes.

Vines give way to woods as the train crisscrosses the milky, rushing waters of the Dranse, with the peaceful valley views switching between left and right. At Sembrancher, where the Orsières branch peels off, the valley widens out so that mountains are visible properly for the first time.

The best view comes on the right as you approach Le Châble, with the deep V of the mountain sides leading down to the church spire at the centre. In contrast, the branch to Orsières has less drama until you reach the terminus, where the lofty peaks are finally visible – a taste of what might have been if the line had continued.

THE HISTORY

Switching tracks at Sembrancher station in July 1954.

The first part to be built was the branch to Orsières, with the concession granted in 1906 to the Martigny-Orsières Railway. Construction began a year later and by 1 September 1910 the first trains were running along the 19km of track. But it was originally planned for the line to carry on to Aosta in Italy via the Great St Bernard pass. Sadly, that never happened so the line simply ends.

Over 40 years later, the 6km-long branch to Le Châble was built by the same railway company. It opened on 5 August 1953 and served as the principal route for construction materials needed for the Mauvoisin Dam. That was finished in 1958, and at 250m tall, is the highest arch dam in Europe. Both branches were electric from the start and since 2001 have been operated by TMR (Transports de Martigny et Régions), along with the nearby Mont-Blanc Express.

EASTERN SWITZERLAND

Bernina Express

28 BERNINA EXPRESS

A masterpiece of technical expertise that runs through spectacular mountain landscapes: not to be missed!

Welcome to one of my favourite Swiss train rides. The scenery is as impressive as anywhere in Switzerland but also the feat of engineering needed to build this line is incredible. Whether it's crossing the lofty Landwasser Viaduct straight into a cliffside tunnel or climbing up to 2253m without cogs, this is a train trip to remember. With 196 bridges, 55 tunnels and countless bends, it's no wonder that this route, built well over a century ago, became a Unesco World Heritage Site in 2008.

This remarkable trip is two separate lines combined into one official panoramic train ride. So, this chapter is divided into two sections, one per line, as both are great – you can enjoy them individually on regular trains or together in the Panorama Express. The first part, the Albula Line, winds through the mountains south of Chur while the second leg, the Bernina Line, climbs up through the Alps then down to Tirano in Italy. The whole route is operated by Rhaetian Railway.

FAST FACTS

START
Chur

END
Tirano

DISTANCE
144km

TIME NEEDED
4h 21min

HEIGHT DIFFERENCE
1824m

WHERE TO SIT
On the right

PASSES
GA & Swiss Travel Pass: free;
Half Fare card: 50% discount

NEARBY LINES
Glacier Express 21
Chur–Arosa 32
Engadin Line 33

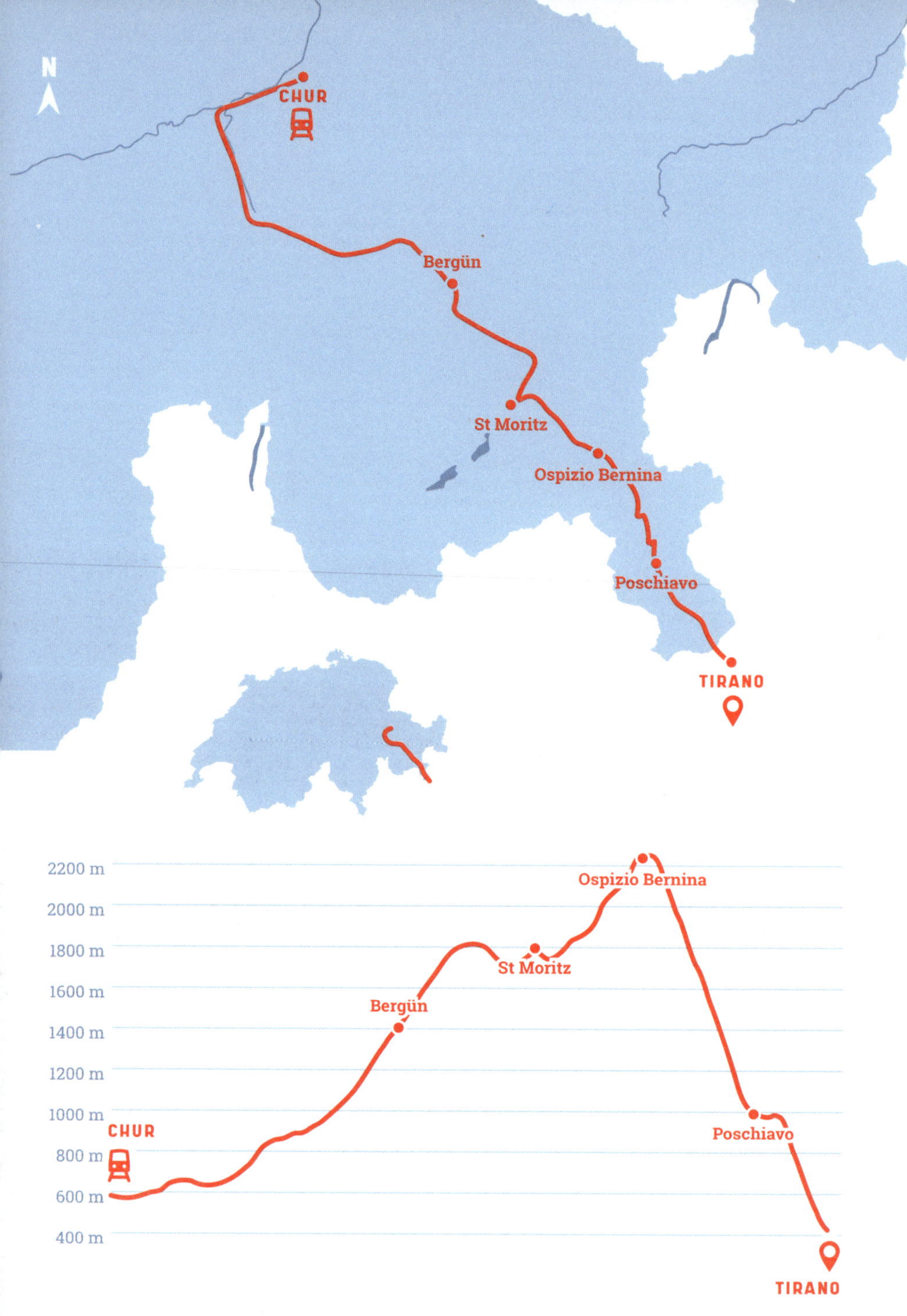
N
CHUR
Bergün
St Moritz
Ospizio Bernina
Poschiavo
TIRANO
2200 m
2000 m
1800 m
1600 m
1400 m
1200 m
1000 m
800 m
600 m
400 m
CHUR
Ospizio Bernina
St Moritz
Bergün
Poschiavo
TIRANO

TRIP TIPS

Taking the official Panorama Express means no changing trains in St Moritz and the carriages having giant picture windows. But I love the normal trains, especially ones with older carriages with windows that open: great for taking photos as the train curls round the bends. Better yet, the open-air carriages that are used in summer.

If you do take the Panorama Express, note that seat reservations are mandatory, even if you have a GA or Swiss Travel Pass. You can reserve seats online or at a ticket office up to three months before the date of travel. Try to reserve seats on the right-hand side facing forwards when going south from Chur.

Such a scenic route through the Alps also has hiking paths, and my favourite is the Albula Railway Adventure Trail. It runs parallel to the Albula Line so you see all the viaducts and loops up close. It's 21km but in one day you can easily do the section northwards from Preda to Bergün, ending up in the fascinating Railway Museum.

ALBULA LINE

For many train fans, this is one of the world's best railway lines, as it combines dramatic mountain scenery with equally dramatic engineering. Opened in 1903, it's still wowing passengers today.

THE ROUTE

Running beside the Rhine from Chur, there's no hint of what's to come. It's only after Thusis, where the line enters the Albula Valley, that the excitement begins. As the valley gets narrower and steeper, the railway must master the landscape, with elaborate constructions, such as the 11-arch Solis Viaduct.

That's merely an appetiser for the main course, one of the most famous bridges in Switzerland: the Landwasser Viaduct (pictured below). At 65m high, 122m long and supported by five towering arches, it almost defies belief that this was built. The bridge ends abruptly at a cliff face so that the train goes straight into a tunnel – pure drama! Sit at the back of the train on the right for the full effect.

Onwards from Bergün, you can relish how the railway curls and loops round, using long bridges and spiral tunnels to crisscross the river and gain height. It's almost as if the majestic scenery takes second place to the human achievement. And then you're plunged into the darkness of the Albula Tunnel, a centrepiece of the line and also its highest point at 1821m. From here, the official Bernina Express heads directly south but the regular service goes to nearby St Moritz, where you can change trains to carry on.

THE HISTORY

The Albula Line features in both the Bernina Express and the Glacier Express (p. 128) but it's the same line with the same history.

Before the Albula Line was built, it was a hard slog to reach the Engadin. A 14-hour coach ride from Chur to St Moritz wasn't exactly conducive to comfortable travel, let alone transporting goods. Once the railway had reached Thusis in 1896, construction began on the line through the mountains just two years later. But it wasn't easy. Not only was the topography challenging but simply getting the materials to the sites was daunting, even though locally quarried limestone was used to build the viaducts. Every section was meticulously planned and built to a precise timetable.

Excavating the Albula Tunnel was particularly strenuous but the final breakthrough came in 1902, precipitating a fast completion of the line, which finally opened to great acclaim on 1 July 1903 (although St Moritz wasn't connected until a year later). It's stayed much the same since then, apart from electrification in 1919 and the new 5.9km-long Albula Tunnel II that opened in 2024. By the way, the Albula Line holds the world record for longest passenger train – in 2022, Rhaetian Railway ran a train with 100 carriages, reaching a total length of 1.9km.

The Landwasser Viaduct under construction in 1901.

BERNINA LINE

It looks like a mountain train and acts like a mountain train, as it clambers up over the Bernina Pass and down into Italy, but this is Europe's highest rail line operating without cogs.

THE ROUTE

Unless you're on the Bernina Express through-train from Chur, your journey over the pass begins in ritzy St Moritz. And it's quite gentle at first, rolling through the lush Engadin Valley surrounded by rugged peaks. Then you start to climb, first past the once-mighty Morteratsch Glacier then up to a wide-open wild landscape at the base of Diavolezza, a mountain easily reached in a side trip by cable car.

The most spectacular section is around Ospizio Bernina, the highest point of the line at 2253m, as the train curls around Lago Bianco then winds downhill to Alp Grüm. This tiny station stands opposite the Palü Glacier (pictured left) so sit on the right for the best views, or maybe even get out at Ospizio and hike down to Alp Grüm.

From then on, navigating the sharp switchbacks downhill results in widescreen valley views that flip from left to right and back again until you reach Poschiavo, a town with Italian flair and great gelato. The last hurrah is the amazing 360° spiral loop of the Brusio Viaduct, built to help the train lose altitude so it can descend into Tirano in Italy. From May to October, you can extend the trip across to Lugano, though only by bus.

THE HISTORY

Driving through a canyon of snow in 1920.

Building the highest transalpine railway crossing was never going to be simple. Inhospitable landscape, remote locations and high altitude all combined to challenge the engineers – no wonder the Bernina Line was built in sections. The easiest parts (Pontresina to Morteratsch and Poschiavo to Tirano) both opened in 1908 but the steep curves of the final section took another two years. On 5 July 1910, one of the steepest adhesion railways in the world (with a maximum incline of 7%) opened after four years of construction.

A small private company, the Bernina Railway, had achieved a monumental goal, especially as the whole line was electric from the start. It was initially only intended for use during the summer (in winter, it was replaced by a sleigh service along the high-altitude sections) but that changed in 1914 with the first year-round timetable. High construction and running costs meant that the Bernina Railway struggled to find a sound financial footing and it faced bankruptcy. The company was taken over in 1943 by Rhaetian Railway, which still operates the line.

29 VORALPEN-EXPRESS

The long-distance trip with a taste of everything: lakes, mountains, cities, villages and very Swiss scenery.

Welcome aboard the Swiss panorama train ride that rarely makes the headlines or tourist itineraries. And that's one reason why I like it. Rather than taking you past giant mountains and mighty glaciers, it wanders languidly through the undulating foothills between Lucerne and St Gallen. This is the calm side of picture-perfect Switzerland, a journey through the verdant heart of the country, alongside lakes and past villages, but with mountains on the horizon; this is still Switzerland.

As well as linking two of the country's finest cities, the Voralpen-Express also gives you the chance to stop off in pretty towns like Rapperswil, ride over Switzerland's highest railway viaduct, cross Lake Zurich on a causeway and travel through the largest Swiss moor. The copper-coloured train's name is relatively new, dating only from 1992, but there's plenty of history in the towns and countryside along the way. It's a local train that goes across the country.

FAST FACTS

START
Lucerne

DISTANCE
125km

HEIGHT DIFFERENCE
525m

PASSES
GA & Swiss Travel Pass: free;
Half Fare card: 50% discount

END
St Gallen

TIME NEEDED
2h 16min

WHERE TO SIT
On the right

NEARBY LINES
Rigi 14
St Gallen–Schaffhausen 31
Gossau–Wasserauen 34

N
ST GALLEN
Herisau
LAKE ZURICH
Rappersswil
LAKE ZUG
Arth-Goldau
LUCERNE
LAKE LUCERNE

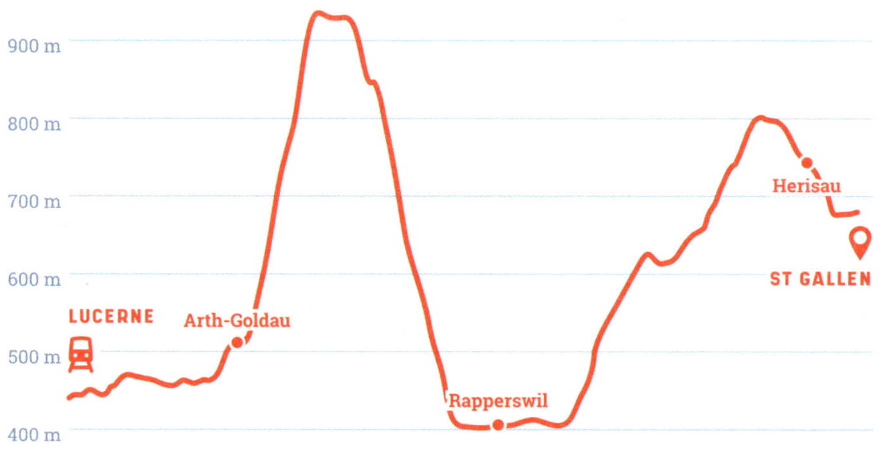
900 m
800 m
700 m
600 m
500 m
400 m
LUCERNE
Arth-Goldau
Rapperswil
Herisau
ST GALLEN

THE ROUTE

From Lucerne's Swiss Transport Museum (one of my favourites) the line skirts along the edge of the lake, with the bulk of Mount Rigi on the right. In fact the train makes a wide semi-circle around Rigi to reach Lake Zug and Arth-Goldau. With the two Mythen peaks on the right, it then slowly climbs through a quintessential Swiss landscape of villages amid fertile farmland and the wooded foothills of the Alps.

That changes once the railway crosses over the Hochmoor, Switzerland's largest high moor. Here the left-hand views are more open, across a wide plateau of peat bogs and reed meadows teeming with protected wildlife. It's a calmly beautiful spot, even from the bubble of your train carriage. From that high point, it's down to Lake Zurich, crossed via a long causeway beside a wooden footbridge, with a grandstand view of Rapperswil Castle on the left.

Head on past the glittering waters of Obersee, with taller peaks on the horizon, before plunging into a long tunnel. Emerging into the lush hills of Toggenburg, look out for the hilltop castle at Wattwil and medieval town of Lichtensteig, both on the left. The final flourish is crossing the Sitter Viaduct – at 99m tall, it's he highest rail bridge in Switzerland. Last stop: St Gallen.

THE HISTORY

Ice creams and magazines on sale on a Lucerne station platform in 1954.

This is a line with both a short and long history: short because it has only existed with the name Voralpen-Express since 1992, long because the oldest section of track opened in 1859 (between Rapperswil and Uznach). Even as a direct connection between eastern and central Switzerland, it progressed in stages, with different train companies involved. Creating such a cross-country route began in earnest in 1904 with the founding of the Bodensee-Toggenburg Railway and the start of construction two years later. With the completion of the crucial link between Uznach and St Gallen, the route opened in October 1910.

Directly connecting Romanshorn on Lake Constance with Rapperswil on Lake Zurich was good but not far enough. Next came eliminating the changes of train need to reach Lucerne: that happened in 1949. This 'Direct Line' was jointly run by the SBB with the Bodensee-Toggenburg Railway and the Südostbahn. A regular two-hourly timetable followed in 1982, although that meant cutting the buffet car, and the new name 10 years later. The Bodensee-Toggenburg Railway merged with the Südostbahn in 2001, and the latter is now the sole operator of the route – which today starts or ends in St Gallen rather than Romanshorn.

TRIP TIPS

At Arth-Goldau you can switch to one of the best mountain train trips in Switzerland, and certainly the oldest (see p. 88). The train up to the summit of Rigi has been running since 1873 and it still wows passengers with its views, most notably the 360° panorama from the top. Definitely one not to miss.

Rapperswil couldn't be more appealing if it tried. A lakeside setting, an attractive old town, a fairytale castle and secluded monastery all combine to make it the jewel of Lake Zurich, even though the town is actually in Canton St Gallen.

A medieval centre packed with ornate oriel windows, a grandiose abbey and a spectacular ancient library makes St Gallen a great destination for history lovers. Don't miss the monumentally impressive station, built from 1911–13. It's a lasting legacy of when the city was booming as a centre of the textile industry.

30 AARE LINTH

Cross-country route between Bern and Chur showcasing a cross-section of Switzerland's urban and rural treasures.

As befits a train ride that slices through half the country in a wide arc, this route has a little bit of everything: it stops in big cities and small towns, slides beside lakes and along rivers and snakes through the foothills to reach the mountains. There are quicker ways to travel this route but sometimes slower is better. No changing trains, no worrying about timetables, no stress – just sit back and watch Switzerland glide past the window.

Travelling by train from the capital of Switzerland to the capital of Graubünden was possible as early as 1875, though not without changing trains along the way. The two main line routes – Bern-Zurich and Zurich-Chur – were well-used from the start, but combining them into one seamless journey with its own name came much later. The first Aare Linth service, named after two rivers but more properly known as InterRegio 35, was inaugurated in December 2021.

FAST FACTS

START
Bern

END
Chur

DISTANCE
236km

TIME NEEDED
3h 7min

HEIGHT DIFFERENCE
211m

WHERE TO SIT
Right then left towards Chur

PASSES
GA & Swiss Travel Pass: free;
Half Fare card: 50% discount

NEARBY LINES
Bern–Geneva 4
Gotthard Railway 26
Voralpen-Express 29

N
Zurich
Olten
LAKE ZURICH
LAKE WALEN
BERN
CHUR

CHUR
600 m
BERN
550 m
500 m
450 m
Zurich
400 m
Olten
350 m

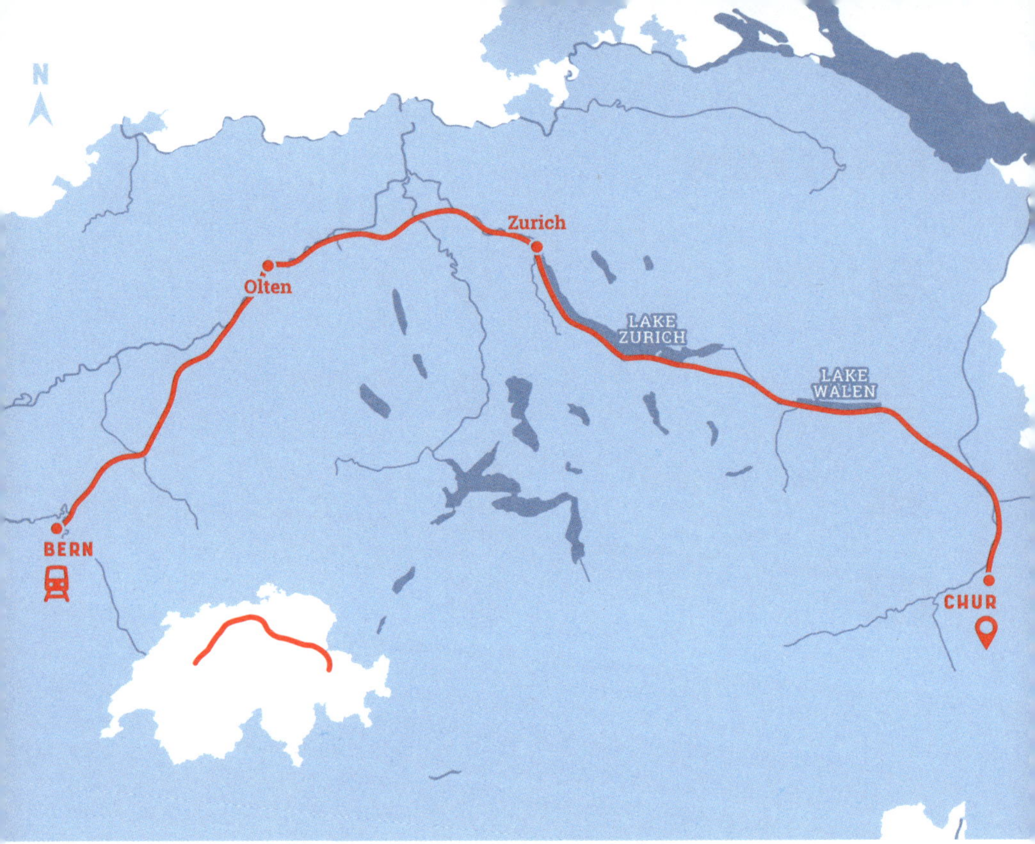

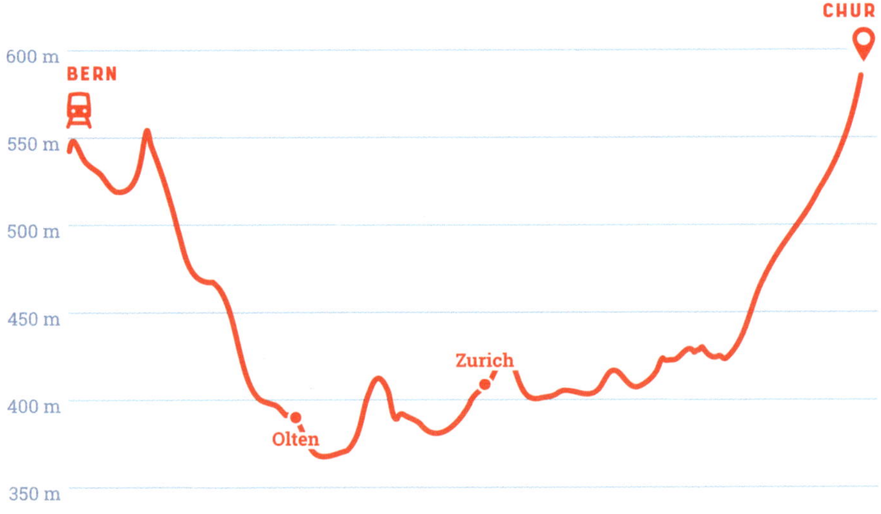

THE ROUTE

For the first half of the journey, it's worth sitting on the right. As the copper-coloured train leaves Bern and crosses the Aare, there's a perfect view of the old town backed by the Alps (on a clear day). Then comes the hilltop castle at Burgdorf, another one at Aarburg and a third at Lenzburg, all on the right.

In between the towns and castles is a gentle landscape of cultivated fields, red-roofed farmhouses, little villages and the train's namesake river (the longest entirely within Switzerland). Switching to the Limmat valley, things become much more urban and industrial on the approach to Switzerland's biggest city, Zurich. From there, sit on the left for the most scenic part of the trip alongside two lakes: Zurich and Walen.

The railway hugs the southern shore of both, giving you water's edge views for most of the time. Connecting the two lakes is the flat plain of the River Linth, but the skyline is then anything but flat. Sheer cliffs tower over the mirror-like waters of Lake Walen before the view opens up again in the broad Rhine Valley. Journey's end is Chur, gateway to the mountains of Graubünden.

THE HISTORY

Chur station in 1954 complete with a Postbus.

It might have a new name and modern marketing, but the Aare Linth service uses some of the oldest railway routes in Switzerland. As it approaches Zurich along the left bank of the River Limmat, it partly follows the course of the first railway line in Switzerland, the Spanisch-Brötli-Bahn. That opened to great fanfare in August 1847, running from Zurich to Baden and laying the groundwork for more Swiss railways. In the time before SBB, lines were built by private companies, often competing against each other for the best routes.

The Swiss Central Railway, founded in Basel in 1853, built the line from Bern to Aarau. At the same time, the Swiss Northeastern Railway was busy extending its railway from Baden to Aarau. When both were complete in November 1858, it was possible to take a train from Bern to Zurich for the first time. Meanwhile, the United Swiss Railways was constructing a line from Ziegelbrücke to Chur, which opened in 1859. The final link along Lake Zurich was finished in September 1875, thanks to the Swiss Northeastern Railway (again). Almost exactly 146 years later, on 12 December 2021, the Aare Linth ran for the first time, but now operated by Südostbahn.

TRIP TIPS

One crucial interchange is Olten, where this east-west service crosses with the north-south Treno Gottardo. This was the original starting point for measuring distances on the whole Swiss rail network, and there's still a stone '0' marker on platform 12: a tiny piece of Swiss train history.

Fancy a break from train travel? Then get off in Zurich and switch to a boat for a section of the journey. It takes a relaxed 2½ hours to sail the length of Lake Zurich to the medieval town of Rapperswil, then a short hop across the water to Pfäffikon SZ, where you can rejoin the Aare Linth train going south.

The Rhine Valley section of the journey has three reasons for you to get off and explore: the spa resort of Bad Ragaz, definitely worth a visit if you want to pamper yourself; the lovely town of Maienfeld, home to the Heidi story (and all the tourists who come to visit); and the vineyards and wineries of the Bündner Herrschaft (pictured below).

31 ST GALLEN ↔ SCHAFFHAUSEN

A local line connecting the towns along Lake Constance and the Rhine that almost touches the German border.

There are some trains rides in Switzerland where it doesn't matter so much where you sit as the views are all around. And then there are lines like this one, where sitting on the wrong side means missing the best bits. Travelling from St Gallen, sit on the right to enjoy the calm of Lake Constance and the River Rhine. It's only as the train trundles into Schaffhausen that you get a great photo moment on the left.

Forget about soaring mountains or deep ravines, this is a route that reveals a real picture of the Switzerland where most of the population lives, works and relaxes. Farms with marshalled lines of apple trees, smart houses along the lakeside, light industry around the towns and quiet villages rarely seen by tourists. And almost the whole way, you're never far from the water, gently flowing northwards.

FAST FACTS

START
St Gallen

END
Schaffhausen

DISTANCE
89km

TIME NEEDED
1h 54min

HEIGHT DIFFERENCE
271m

WHERE TO SIT
On the right

PASSES
GA & Swiss Travel Pass: free;
Half Fare card: 50% discount

NEARBY LINES
Aare Linth 30
Voralpen-Express 29
Gossau–Wasserauen 34

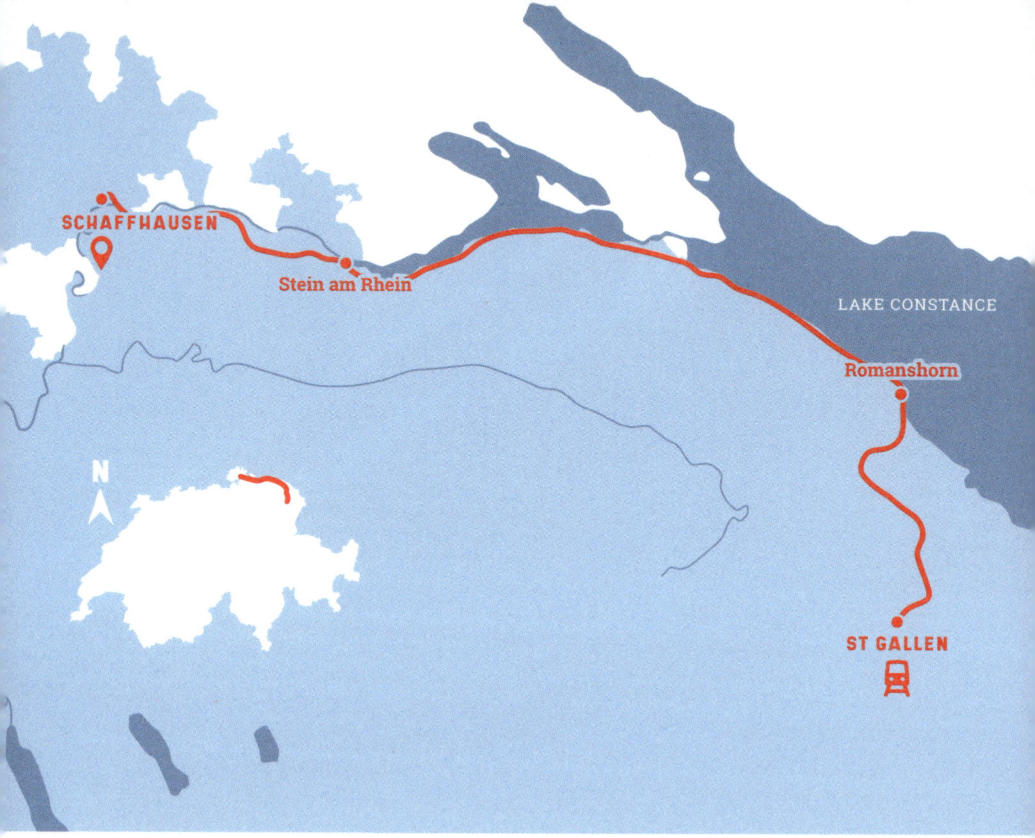

SCHAFFHAUSEN
Stein am Rhein
LAKE CONSTANCE
Romanshorn
ST GALLEN
N

ST GALLEN
700 m
650 m
600 m
550 m
500 m
450 m
400 m
Romanshorn
Stein am Rhein
SCHAFFHAUSEN

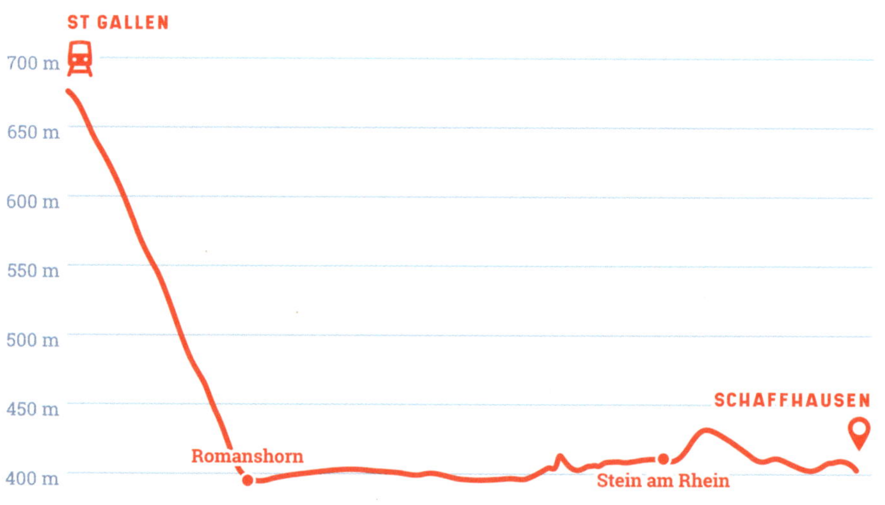

THE ROUTE

This is an S-Bahn, or suburban railway, that's also a direct connection between two cities that are almost 90km apart. That means a lot of stops along the way, and the third stop brings the first glimpse of Lake Constance. Between the orchards around Roggwil-Berg, the vast expanse of water shimmers with the hills of Germany behind.

Apples are a big deal in Thurgau and they're everywhere to be seen, or at least their trees are. Mostly in regimented rows like giant vineyards but also more rustically romantic as proper trees spaced apart. None to be seen at all in Romanshorn, which instead has a busy working port with ferries and sailboats. From here, the railway hugs the lakeshore all the way to the border town of Kreuzlingen, and then on past the smaller Untersee part of this huge lake.

As the lake narrows to become a river, Germany gets ever closer until you can almost reach out and touch the half-timbered houses across the border. This is a tranquil corner of the country, with villages tucked in between wooded hills and flatter farmland. Then, the line crosses the Rhine for the first time and on the left is Schaffhausen with its mighty Munot fortress dominating the skyline.

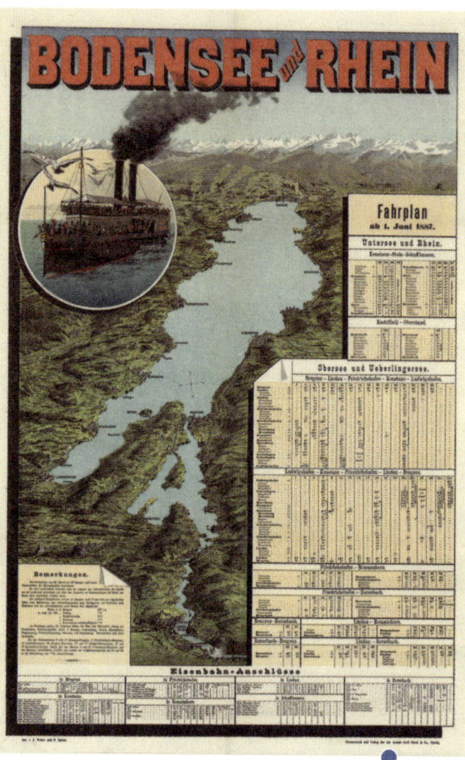

Poster of Lake Constance from June 1887 showing both train and boat timetables.

THE HISTORY

Most of this line was built by the Swiss Northeastern Railway, a powerhouse of a railway company that dominated in the eastern part of Switzerland. It was founded in Zurich in 1853 and at its peak was the largest railway company in Switzerland. The man in charge was Alfred Escher, the banker and industrialist who championed building the Gotthard railway and tunnel. This line was less of a challenge than that grand project, at least in geographical terms. The Swiss Northeastern Railway eventually became an integral part of the SBB upon its creation in 1902.

The first section along the lakeshore was built relatively early, with the grand opening on 1 July 1871, linking Romanshorn with Kreuzlingen and on further to Stein am Rhein. The connection to Schaffhausen took a while longer – in November 1894 came an initial extension along the south bank of the Rhine. The final link to Schaffhausen required the construction of the Feuerthalen bridge over the river and the 761m-long Emmersberg tunnel under the Munot; both finally opened on 2 April 1895. At the other end of this route, the railway from St Gallen to Romanshorn was built as part of a cross-country route (see Voralpen-Express, p. 184), and was completed in October 1910.

TRIP TIPS

Constance is not in Switzerland but I'll make an exception as it's a beautiful city with an impressive cathedral. Get off in Kreuzlingen and either walk or catch a local train over the border into Germany. The odd thing is that the historic old town of Constance actually lies on the 'Swiss' (i.e. southern) bank of the Rhine.

Stein am Rhein is easily one of Switzerland's most attractive towns. The compact centre is a kaleidoscope of painted houses, colourful murals, elaborate frescoes and sumptuous 'sgraffito'. In contrast to Constance, here the Swiss town is on the 'German' or northern side of the Rhine but is only a short walk from the station.

In Schaffhausen you can change trains and carry on to Zurich. The main line passes right by the Rhine Falls so sit on the left for a perfect view of Europe's largest waterfalls. Or take a local train and get off at Schloss Laufen am Rheinfall to see the roaring water up close.

32 CHUR ↔ AROSA

Take a ride on the wild side up the rugged Schanfigg valley to the high-altitude resort deep in Graubünden.

The dramatic railway to Arosa is a classic case of a line being built for one purpose: tourism. There was little demand for a train line, as almost no one lived in Arosa and even fewer took the trouble to visit. That changed with tourism, and you could argue that in Arosa's case, it was all down to health. What started as a quest for fresh air became a desire for outdoor activities, and a means for a railway to prosper.

In the last years of the 19th century, Arosa found fame as a mountain spa resort in competition with nearby Davos. Back then, spas weren't for being pampered with seaweed wraps – they were all about using the clean, thin air to recover from illnesses like tuberculosis. This health tourism was a year-round business, and one that needed good transport links. Today, the railway might be packed with hikers and skiers but it was originally built to take invalids up to the mountains to be cured.

FAST FACTS

START
Chur

END
Arosa

DISTANCE
26km

TIME NEEDED
1h 1min

HEIGHT DIFFERENCE
1155m

WHERE TO SIT
On the right going up

PASSES
GA & Swiss Travel Pass: free; Half Fare card: 50% discount

NEARBY LINES
Glacier Express 21
Bernina Express 28
Landquart–Filisur 35

THE ROUTE

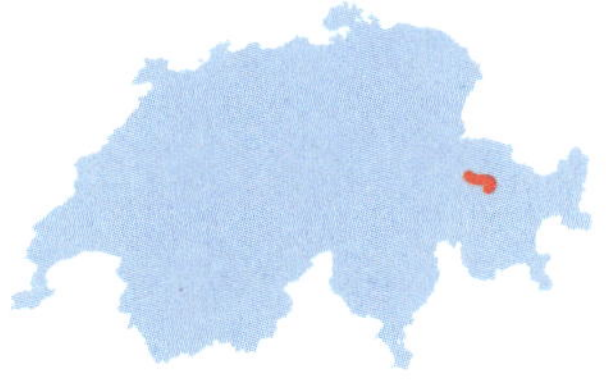

It begins as a giant tram trundling through the streets of Chur, with the first stop (on request) at the Altstadt itself. Then the train heads into a gorge, and from here on the views are all on the right. This isn't a rack railway but it feels steep, especially as the tracks climb up one side of the valley with sheer drops off to the right.

The landscape is weird and wonderful: huge stony ridges interlocking at angles, waterfalls tumbling down rocks, brief glimpses of the river far below and wooden stations seemingly in the middle of nowhere. In summer it's 50 shades of green, from fresh ferns to dark conifers; in winter it's a white wonderland.

The line's centrepiece is the enormous Langwieser Viaduct (287m long and 62m high, pictured below), the world's first railway bridge to be built from reinforced concrete. It straddles the River Plessur, giving splendid views on both sides as you cross. With big, wide curves, the train gains altitude, finally stopping amid the rocky peaks around Arosa.

THE HISTORY

The Langwieser Viaduct under construction in 1913.

Back in 1870 Arosa had a mere 61 inhabitants and few visitors. Then the road from Chur opened and the boom began, although it was soon clear that the road couldn't cope with the volume of traffic. So a railway was planned. And revised. And re-worked. Finally, things began happening in 1911 with the foundation of the Chur Arosa Railway Company. Construction started in the summer of 1912 but it wasn't easy, thanks to the challenging landscape.

The topography necessitated 19 tunnels plus 52 bridges and viaducts, making this line one of the most expensive per kilometre in Graubünden. It was built as a metre-gauge railway with a maximum gradient of 6% and was electrified from the start. On 12 December 1914 the first passengers used the newly completed line and the inter-war rise in winter tourism helped fuel the railway's success. It didn't last. The company ran into difficulties and was taken over by Rhaetian Railway in 1942.

33 ENGADIN LINE

Travel along one of the most beautiful valleys in Switzerland, amid unspoilt scenery and bathed in sunshine.

When you need to escape to a place where you're surrounded by nature, a place where the light is as clean as the air, then come to the Engadin. This high-altitude valley of the River Inn really is as lovely as the marketing hype makes out – and it can be enjoyed from the train. Yes, it's a magnet for those who love the outdoors but sometimes it's equally pleasing to sit back while the beauty rolls by your window.

Although this line mainly runs through the narrower Lower Engadin, it starts/ends in the wider Upper Engadin. Direct services run between Pontresina and Scuol-Tarasp, but it's also easy to begin in St Moritz and switch trains in Samedan. It may not be as high-profile as other Rhaetian Railway routes, but its craggy mountains and pristine environment make it a crowd-pleaser, even though it's rarely ever crowded. A true local delight.

FAST FACTS

START
Pontresina

END
Scuol-Tarasp

DISTANCE
57km

TIME NEEDED
1h 25min

HEIGHT DIFFERENCE
487m

WHERE TO SIT
On the right

PASSES
GA & Swiss Travel Pass: free;
Half Fare card: 50% discount

NEARBY LINES
Glacier Express 21
Bernina Express 28
Landquart–Filisur 35

N
SCUOL-TARASP
Guarda
Bever
PONTRESINA

PONTRESINA
1800 m
Bever
1700 m
1600 m
1500 m
1400 m
Guarda
1300 m
SCUOL-TARASP

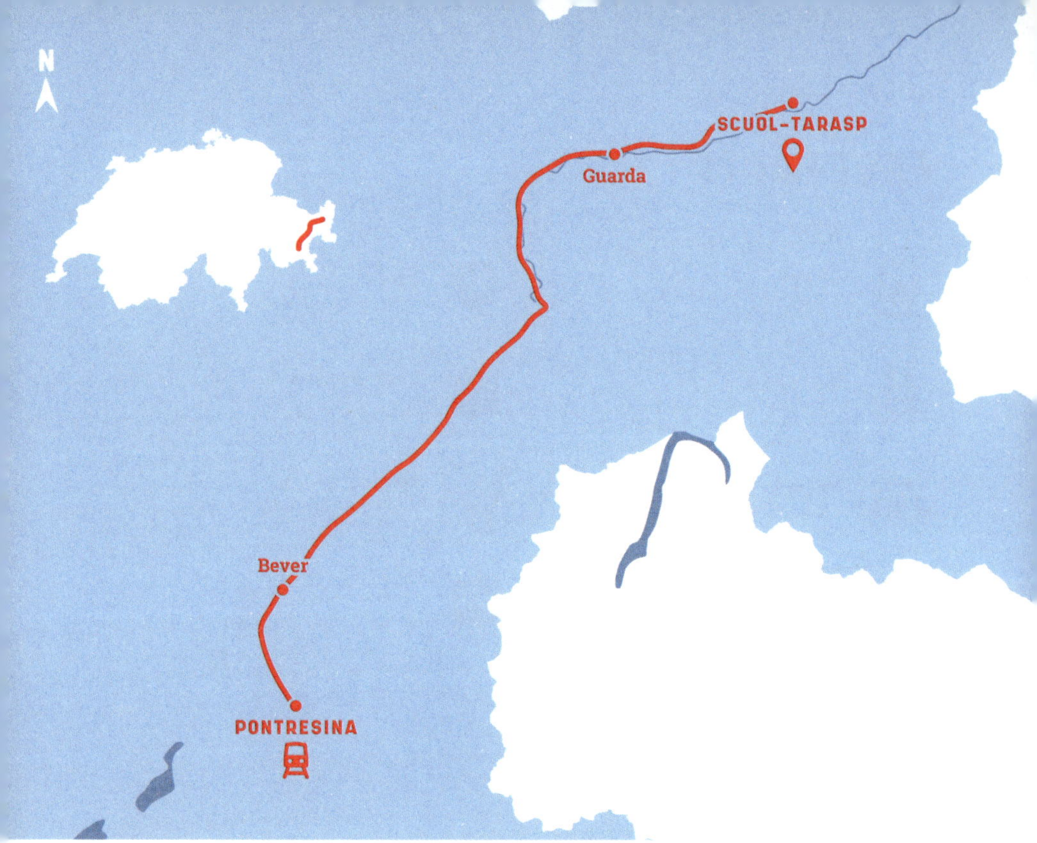

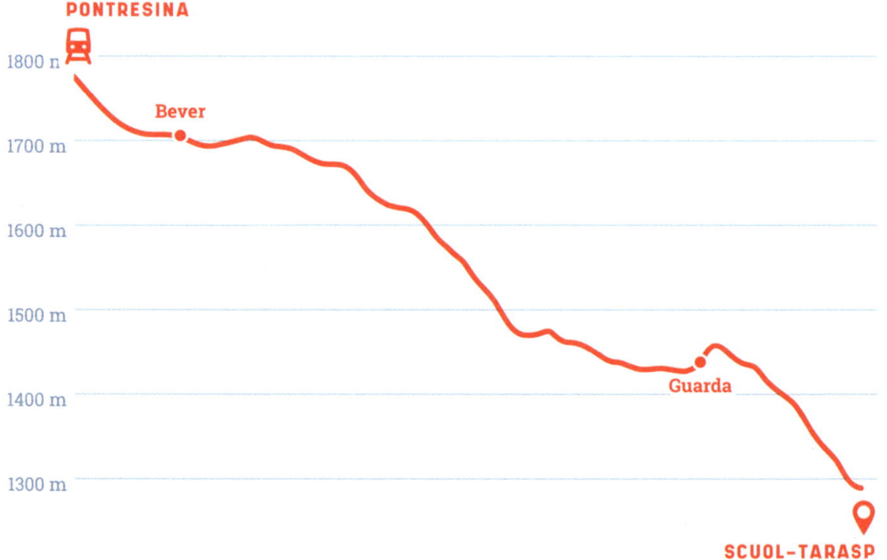

THE ROUTE

Heading north from Pontresina, the railway initially follows the River Flaz on its way to merge with the Inn at Samedan. Conical hills on either side accentuate the flat bottoms of both valleys, making an almost magical landscape despite this being the more developed end of the Engadin. Announcements are in Romansh, then German, then English: you're definitely in deepest Graubünden here.

After Bever, where the Albula Line branches off to Chur, the views are on the right as the valley gradually narrows while the hills get more rugged. Thousands of fir trees populate the ever-steeper slopes while the milky river is ever present as the railway slowly climbs upwards. The only downside is that it's hard to see the impressive engineering beneath the train's wheels, such as the arches of the Val Mela Viaduct.

Switch to the left before coming round the giant bend at Zernez for views of the town backed by mighty peaks such as Piz Linard. Then it's back to the right so you can look down the steep cliffs to the River Inn, now far below our feet. The grandstand view of Tarasp Castle, perched high on its rock, comes both before and after the long Tasna Tunnel. And then it's over: the end of the line in the spa town of Scuol.

THE HISTORY

Photo from 1920 of the Val Püzza Viaduct with Tarasp Castle behind.

Given that it follows the course of a major river, you might think that the Engadin Line was one of the earlier, easier railways to be built in Graubünden. Think again. It was one of the last projects during the boom of railway construction before the First World War. The main section from Bever to Scuol was opened by Rhaetian Railway on 1 July 1913, by which time trains had been running along the sinuous Albula Line from Chur for a full 10 years. As for the plans for this line to carry on eastwards to Landeck in Austria or Merano in Italy, they never came to fruition.

The metre-gauge line was planned as an electric railway from the start, quite a pioneering feat for a high Alpine railway. Not forgetting the 79 bridges and 17 tunnels that Friedrich Hennings, the German engineer who had designed the Albula Line, planned along the route. Construction was plagued with difficulties, such as bridge collapses and tunnelling problems, so that it overran by a year. Most of the 2500 workers were Italian, with 25 of them sadly dying during construction. The opening of the Vereina Tunnel in 1999 provided a direct link from the Lower Engadin to Klosters, and gave new hope to the dream of this line crossing the border.

TRIP TIPS

The first stop after Pontresina is Punt Muragl, the base station for a wonderful funicular ride up to Muottas Muragl. From the top, at 2456m, there's an unparalleled view of the Upper Engadin with its string of glittering lakes sitting between majestic peaks. Lunch on the restaurant terrace is as perfect as things get.

All along the route are typical Engadin villages, where houses have thick walls and deep windows, and are decorated in the traditional 'sgraffito' style. One of the most popular villages to visit is Guarda, sitting up above the valley and the setting for a favourite Swiss children's book, 'A Bell for Ursli'.

Rhaetian Railway has some good-value online tickets that are ideal for hopping on and off trains. You can explore the whole canton with the multi-day Graubünden Pass, or just certain sections of the rail network with special day tickets; for example, the Short Round Trip South ticket includes most of the Engadin Line.

34 GOSSAU ↔ WASSERAUEN

Meander through the hills in two of Switzerland's smallest cantons to reach the mountains.

How do you know you're on a train in Appenzellerland? Simply by looking out the window and spotting the distinctive farmhouses: typically a wooden house with painted façade and the barn attached at right angles. On holidays, your fellow passengers might even be in traditional local dress: the 'Tracht' for women and red waistcoats for men. This is Switzerland for the quaint-hearted, and that includes the train rides.

This metre-gauge railway starts in Gossau, where it intersects with the main line from Zurich, although it is over the border in Canton St Gallen. If you want your trip to be a totally Appenzell experience, then start in Herisau, capital of Appenzell Ausserrhoden. It's also a connection point to the Voralpen-Express, which runs between Lucerne and St Gallen (see p. 184).

FAST FACTS

START
Gossau

DISTANCE
32km

HEIGHT DIFFERENCE
231m

PASSES
GA & Swiss Travel Pass: free;
Half Fare card: 50% discount

END
Wasserauen

TIME NEEDED
51min

WHERE TO SIT
On the left

NEARBY LINES
Voralpen-Express 29
Aare Linth 30
St Gallen–Schaffhausen 31

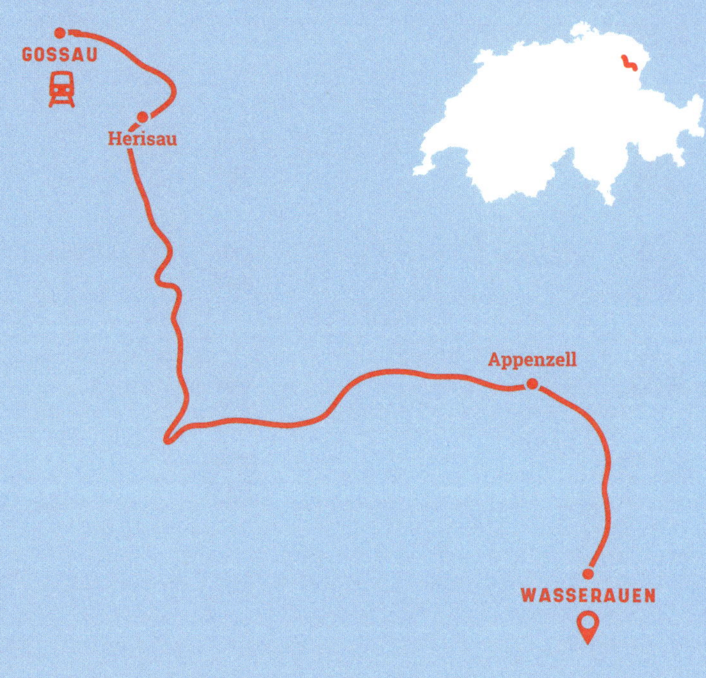
N
GOSSAU
Herisau
Appenzell
WASSERAUEN

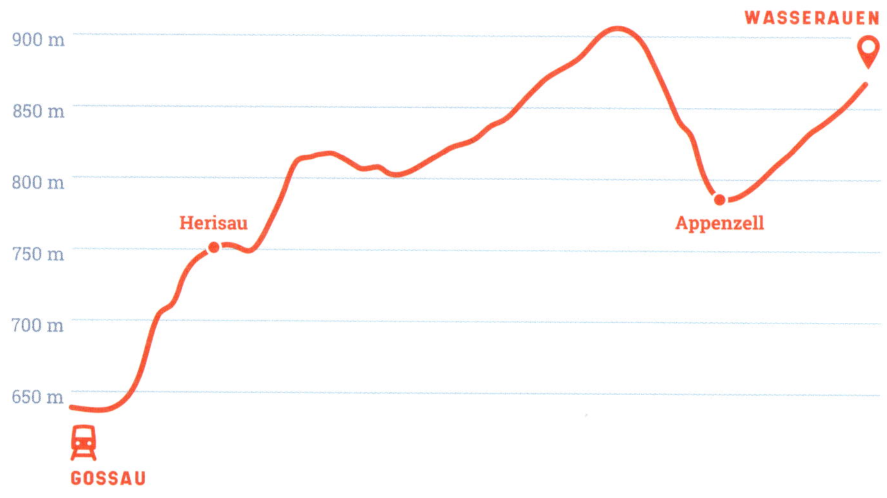
900 m
850 m
800 m
750 m
700 m
650 m
WASSERAUEN
Herisau
Appenzell
GOSSAU

THE ROUTE

Almost straight after leaving Gossau, you pass through fields of cows and sunflowers with undulating hills on the horizon – but it's also a busy corridor along the motorway so expect giant supermarket distribution centres, too. A few minutes down the track is Herisau, though you must get off to see the village's pretty centre.

Rural slowly replaces urban, with hills becoming steeper and farms more common. At Waldstatt the region's big mountain, Säntis, is visible for the first time on the left, and from then on it's the focal point of the views. As the line curls left and right through rolling hills, it gets ever closer, dominating the skyline with its jagged profile.

The hills get more conical and the fields more velvety as the train approaches Appenzell, with broad valley views on the left. As in Herisau, the painted houses aren't visible from the train, so instead stay on board for the dramatic finale. The line heads south, alongside mighty cliffs until it ends at the base of even mightier mountains. This dead-end is mainly for those going up to Ebenalp but it's an imposing end to a gentle train ride.

THE HISTORY

This local line originally started in Winkeln, the westernmost district in the city of St Gallen, and the first section to Herisau opened on 12 April 1875. It was constructed by the Swiss Local Railway Company, which extended the line to Urnäsch in September the same year. The extension to Appenzell was already planned, so that sleepers for the whole line were ordered and delivered: 8000 oak and 24,000 pine, as well as 34,000 bolts. Financial and technical problems delayed the continuation of the railway, compounded by disagreements between the two cantons on how to proceed. Construction finally began in 1885 and was completed in October 1886.

A 1904 poster from SBB advertising the charms of Appenzell.

Trains ran between Winkeln and Appenzell for almost 30 more years before any further progress was made. It was only in July 1912 that the railway was extended to its current terminus at Wasserauen, while a direct connection to St Gallen failed to materialise. Eventually a metre-gauge line was built between Herisau and Gossau, opening in October 1913 and so making the Winkeln-Herisau section defunct (it was dismantled). What had begun as the Swiss Local Railway Company became the Appenzell Railway in 1885 and then through a series of mergers with other local rail companies, became plural: since 1988, it's been Appenzell Railways.

TRIP TIPS

At Urnäsch, the railway makes a giant loop so that the views switch for a while from the left-hand side to the right. It's also the stop to get off if you want to go to the summit of Säntis: switch to a bus for a 20-minute ride to the cable car up. Definitely worth it for the panorama from the top at 2502m.

For the return journey, you could get off at Appenzell, the tiny but picturesque cantonal capital with its muralled buildings and deliciously pungent cheese. From there, take a different branch of Appenzell Railways to reach St Gallen, with its amazing abbey and library, and the main line back to Zurich.

Wasserauen is the jumping off point for exploring the eastern end of the Swiss Alps. Most popular is the cable car up to Ebenalp and then the hike to the Instagram-famous Aescher guesthouse, set into the cliff above the valley. Those with sure feet and steady heads can carry on the steep path to the beautiful Seealpsee.

35 LANDQUART ↔ FILISUR

A slow start that builds to a crescendo of scenery while also connecting two famous Alpine resorts to the outside world.

When this railway first opened in 1890, it was a cul-de-sac with only one destination: Davos. Extending the line to Filisur made it more popular and much more dramatic. A complex bridge-and-tunnel construction was needed to master the many river ravines, some of which you glimpse fleetingly as you emerge from a tunnel to cross a viaduct only to be plunged into darkness again moments later.

Every Swiss train company has to begin somewhere, and Rhaetian Railway began with the line from Landquart to Davos. It is the oldest part of the cantonal rail company, although not at first the most scenic; however, that prize could easily go to the later section west of Davos, which can hold its own against the stiff competition from its more famous neighbours. It's a wild and beautiful ride through the mountains.

FAST FACTS

START
Landquart

END
Filisur

DISTANCE
69km

TIME NEEDED
2h 9min

HEIGHT DIFFERENCE
1102m

WHERE TO SIT
On the right

PASSES
GA & Swiss Travel Pass: free;
Half Fare card: 50% discount

NEARBY LINES
Bernina Express 28
Aare Linth 30
Engadin Line 33

N
LANDQUART
Jenaz
Klosters
Davos
FILISUR

1600 m
1400 m
1200 m
1000 m
800 m
600 m
Davos
Klosters
Jenaz
FILISUR
LANDQUART

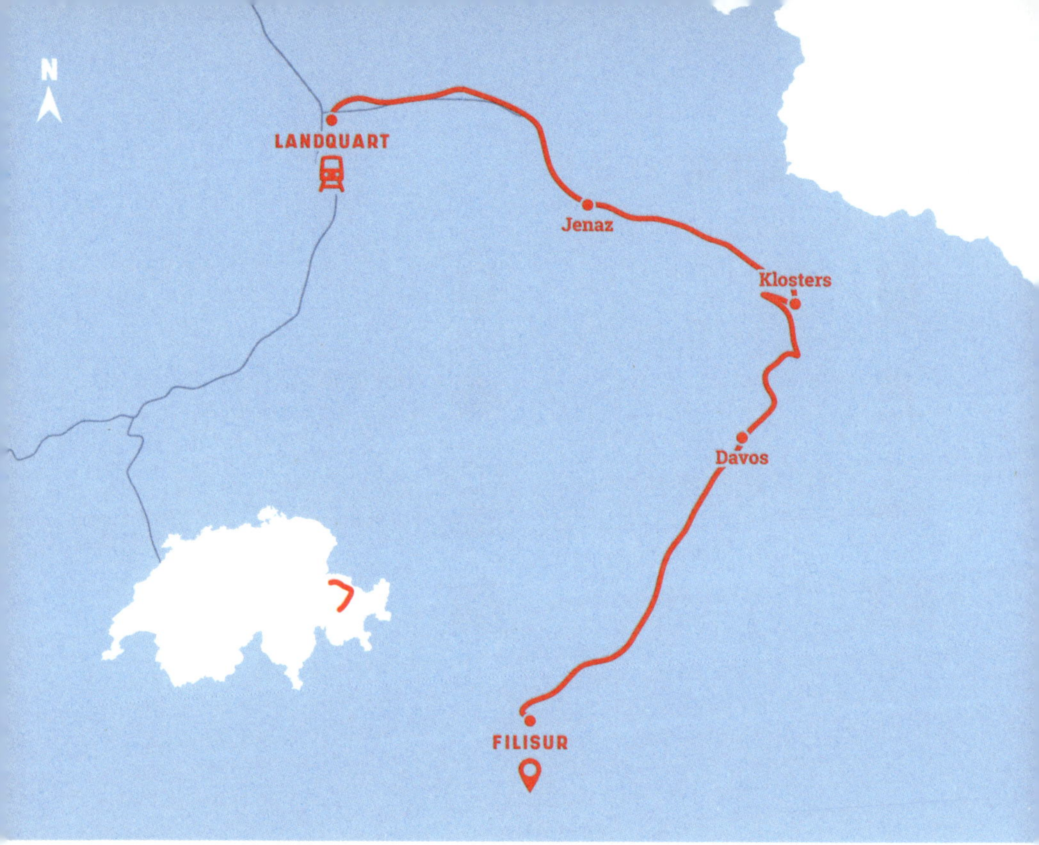

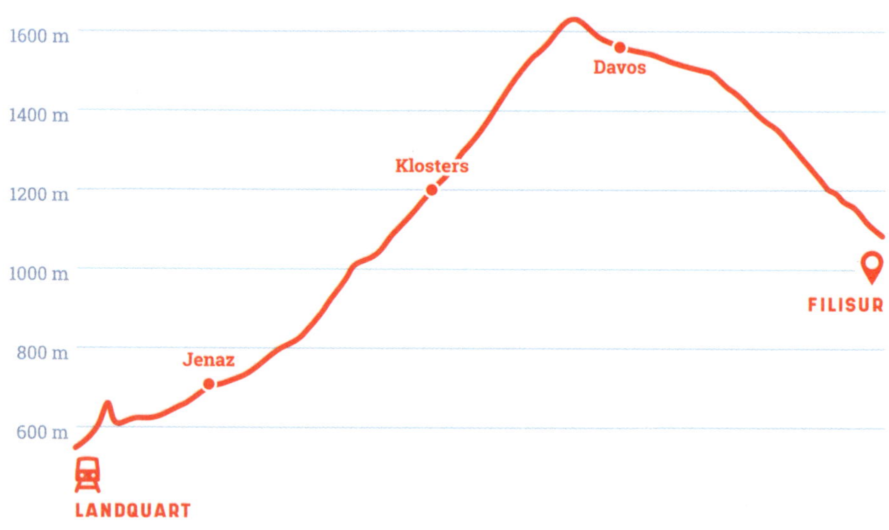

THE ROUTE

It's a gentle start in the broad valley of the Rhine, and the first stretch of the River Landquart is equally flat farmland – until the rails head south then ascend. From Jenaz onwards things get more dramatic, with the railway twisting its way alongside the milky green river between the steep, tree-clad slopes.

Then the first peaks appear on the jagged skyline to the right, giving a taste of what's to come. Check out the impressive Sunniberg road bridge followed by a sweeping curve around Klosters Dorf, with great valley views. After losing half the train at Klosters Platz, the steady climb up to Davos begins via horseshoe tunnels and wide loops. It's an easy change of trains in Davos Platz and you're off again.

It only takes 30 minutes to go through the deep cleft of the River Landwasser, but what a half hour. A parade of waterfalls, cliffs, gorges and trees – and amazing engineering. Look out for the short Brombenz Viaduct, sandwiched between two tunnels and straddling a precipitous gully. The crown jewel of the line is the 210m-long Wiesen Viaduct, one of the largest stone arch bridges in Europe, though sadly it's hard to see when in a train travelling over it. All too soon, you're in Filisur.

THE HISTORY

A 1909 poster by Walter Koch of the impressive Wiesen Viaduct.

A Dutchman was the driving force behind a railway being built up to one of the most famous Swiss resorts. Willem Jan Holsboer, who had moved to Davos in 1867 because of his wife's lung disease, founded the resort's spa association. One of its major infrastructure projects was the construction of the line from Landquart to Klosters and Davos. It was originally intended to be a rack railway but eventually the design became a metre-gauge line with a steepest gradient of 4.5%. Work began in the summer of 1888, with the section to Klosters opening in October 1889. The first trains reached Davos on 21 July 1890.

And there the trains stopped for many years. Going further west was technically and economically challenging, given there was no other line to connect to. That changed with the opening of the Albula Line in 1903, making a link between Davos and Filisur eminently viable. By this time, the Landquart Davos Railway Company had grown and become Rhaetian Railway, which undertook the construction of the missing link that finally opened on 1 July 1909. The whole route from Landquart was electrified in stages, ending in 1921. Plans to connect this line with Arosa have been around for over a century, with the latest version being a tunnel, but they have yet to come to anything.

TRIP TIPS

From May to October there's a delightful way to travel between Davos and Filisur – a vintage train. It runs twice a day in both directions, with carriages from the 1920s (First Class is very plush) plus an open-air one, which is my favourite: wind in your hair, the drama of the tunnels and great for taking photos.

At Filisur you can switch trains to go north to Chur or south to St Moritz. Or you can hike down to stand underneath the famous Landwasser Viaduct and watch the Glacier Express go overhead. If you don't fancy the steep walk down and back up, there's a little tourist train running the same route from Filisur station.

The train leaves Landquart with two destinations on the board and splits in half at Klosters-Platz. Make sure you're in the correct carriage or you'll end up in St Moritz. That direct route to the Engadin was made possible by the opening of the Vereina Tunnel in 1999, transforming the first half of this line into a busy connecting railway.

TIMELINE

Swiss Federal Railways, or SBB, was created on 1 January 1902, so most of these lines were built by private companies.

Lausanne ↔ Biel/Bienne
3 December 1860

Bern ↔ Geneva
4 September 1862

Rigi
27 June 1873

Bern ↔ Lucerne
11 August 1875

Bern ↔ Chur
20 September 1875

Basel ↔ Porrentruy
30 March 1877

Geneva ↔ Brig
1 June 1878

Gotthard Railway
1 June 1882

Brünig Line
14 June 1888

Pilatus
4 June 1889

Monte Generoso
5 June 1890

Bernese Oberland Railway
1 July 1890

Landquart ↔ Davos
21 July 1890

Visp ↔ Zermatt
18 July 1891

Grütschalp ↔ Mürren
14 August 1891

Brienzer Rothorn
17 June 1892

Rochers-de-Naye
28 July 1892

Schynige Platte
14 June 1893

Wengernalp Railway
20 June 1893

Yverdon-les-Bains ↔ Sainte-Croix
27 November 1893

Romanshorn ↔ Schaffhausen
2 April 1895

Lucerne ↔ Rapperswil
1 June 1897

Gornergrat
20 August 1898

Luzern-Engelberg Express
5 October 1898

Albula Line
1 July 1903

Jura Railways
21 May 1904

GoldenPass Line
6 July 1905

Mont-Blanc Express
1 July 1908

Davos ↔ Filisur
1 July 1909

Bernina Line
5 July 1910

St-Bernard Express
1 September 1910

St Gallen ↔ Rapperswil
3 October 1910

Jungfraujoch
1 August 1912

Engadin Line
1 July 1913

Gossau ↔ Wasserauen
1 October 1913

The Lötschberger
15 July 1913

Aigle ↔ Les Diablerets
7 July 1914

Chur ↔ Arosa
12 December 1914

Luzern-Interlaken Express
23 August 1916

Centovalli Railway
25 November 1923

Chur ↔ Brig
4 July 1926

Glacier Express
25 June 1930

Postcard from 1903 with the Eiger Glacier and the 'new' kiosk.

TRAIN PASSES

If you travel often by train, then invest in a travel pass of some kind. Here's an overview of the main passes:

GA TRAVELCARD

The GA (short for 'Generalabonnement' in German) is the principal annual travel pass, valid for unlimited travel on most trains – as well as buses, trams and boats. Typically, mountain trains are not included (though there are exceptions such as Rigi) but instead have a 50% discount. The GA can be bought for First or Second Class but within each class there are also different types of discounted GA Travelcards, such as for Youths (aged 16-25), Seniors or the Duo for two people living in the same household. There's also a GA valid only for one month.

HALF FARE TRAVELCARD

An annual pass that gives you 50% off tickets on most trains (and other forms of public transport) in the whole country. It is the most popular pass, with around a third of the Swiss population owning one. A new Half Fare Plus scheme allows you to deposit money for buying tickets and then receive a bonus credit. Visitors from abroad can buy a regular Half Fare Travelcard for one month.

SWISS TRAVEL PASS

The main pass for visitors from abroad, giving holders the same benefits as the GA Travelcard, including 50% off most mountain trains. It can be bought for First or Second Class and is valid for 3, 4, 6, 8 or 15 consecutive days of travel. The Swiss Travel Pass Flex differs in that the valid days are freely selectable within one month. There are Youth versions of both passes for visitors under 25.

JUNIOR TRAVELCARD

With this annual pass children aged 6 to 16 travel for free when accompanied by at least one parent, who must have a valid ticket. This pass can be used anywhere within the Half Fare Travelcard area of validity.

DAY PASSES

Travel around the whole of Switzerland in one day? No problem, and there are various options for a Day Pass. If you have a Half Fare Travelcard, you can buy a Day Pass at any time for any day. Or there are Supersaver Day Passes (only available online at sbb.ch), available for anyone with or without Half Fare Travelcards but passes are for a specific date. Or some communities also sell the Municipal Day Pass, again for a specific date of travel.

REGIONAL PASSES

Great for one region, with pretty much unlimited use of trains and many mountain railways within a defined area. Some are valid on consecutive days, others limit the free days but give discounts on remaining days. Most are cheaper if you already have a GA, Half Fare Travelcard or Swiss Travel Pass. Popular options include the Berner Oberland Pass, Graubünden Pass, Jungfrau Travel Pass, Lake Geneva-Alps Pass, Matterhorn Gotthard Pass and Tell-Pass Central Switzerland.

OTHER PASSES

The main international passes are valid in Switzerland: for European residents there is Interrail and for non-Europeans, Eurail. With either pass, always check on validity, ticket discounts and seat reservations – especially for panoramic routes and mountain trains.

PHOTO CREDITS

P. 6-7 © Jungfraubahnen
P. 11 © Diccon Bewes
P. 12-25 © MOB, GoldenPass
P. 26-27 © SBB
P. 28 © Andrii Shepeliev/ Shutterstock.com
P. 29 © SBB Historic
P. 30-31 © Shutterstock
P. 33 © Olivier Tanner
P. 34 © SBB Historic
P. 35 © Boris Stroujko/ Shutterstock.com
P. 37 ©Natheepat Kiatpaphaphong Shutterstock.com
P. 39 © Olivier Tanner
P. 40 © SBB Historic
P. 41 © Haidamac/Shutterstock.com
P. 42-43 ©Heying Hua/ Shutterstock.com
P. 44 © Olivier Tanner
P. 45 © SBB Historic
P. 46-48 © Transports publics du Chablais
P. 49 © SBB Historic
P. 51-52 © Les chemins de fer du Jura
P. 53 © SBB Historic
P. 54-56 © Jo Bersier
P. 57 © Travys
P. 58-59 © Rigi Bahnen AG
P. 61-63 © Zentralbahn
P. 64 © Sammlung Joachim Biemann
P. 65 © Zentralbahn
P. 66-71 © Brienz Rothorn Bahn
P. 73-81 © Jungfraubahnen
P. 83 © Pilatus Bahnen AG
P. 84 © Diccon Bewes
P. 85-87 © Pilatus Bahnen AG
P. 88-93 © Rigi Bahnen AG
P. 95 © Jungfraubahnen
P. 96-97 © Diccon Bewes
P. 98 © Jungfraubahnen
P. 99 © Diccon Bewes
P. 100-102 © BLS AG
P. 103 © SBB Historic
P. 105-108 © BLS AG
P. 109 © Rob Lewis Photography
P. 110-113 © Jungfraubahnen
P. 114-117 © Zentralbahn
P. 118 © SBB Historic
P. 119 © Stanserhorn Bahn
P. 120-121 © Gornergrat Bahn
P. 123 © Rob Lewis
P. 125 © Sara Daepp
P. 126 © Centovalli
P. 127 © Christian Guerra
P. 128-129 © Matterhorn Gotthard Bahn

P. 131-132 © RhB, Andrea Badrutt
P. 133 © RhB Archive
P. 134 © RhB, Andrea Badrutt
P. 135 © RhB Archive
P. 136-139 © Matterhorn Gotthard Bahn
P. 141-143 © Mont-Blanc Express
P. 144 © SBB Historic
P. 145 © Diccon Bewes
P. 146-147 © Furka Dampfbahn, Beat Moser
P. 149-151 © DFB-Bildarchiv
P. 152-153 © Gornergrat Bahn
P. 154 © Diccon Bewes
P. 155-156 © Gornergrat Bahn
P. 157 © Gaudenz Danuser
P. 158-163 © Monte Generoso
P. 164-165 © Südostbahn
P. 167 © SBB
P. 168 © SBB Historic
P. 169 © Diccon Bewes
P. 171 © Regionalps
P. 172 © Olivier Tanner
P. 173 © SBB Historic
P. 174-177 © RhB, Andrea Badrutt
P. 179-180 © Diccon Bewes
P. 181 © RhB Archive
P. 182 © RhB, Andrea Badrutt
P. 183 © RhB Archive
P. 184-187 © Südostbahn
P. 188 © SBB Historic
P. 189 © Zurich Tourism
P. 190-193 © Südostbahn
P. 194 © SBB Historic
P. 195 © Heidiland Tourismus, Thomas Kessler
P. 197 © Foto Thurbo
P. 199 © SBB
P. 200 © SBB Historic
P. 201 © Robert Bösch
P. 203 © RhB, Sylvia Heldstab
P. 204 © RhB, Hansjörg Egger
P. 205 © RhB Archive
P. 206-209 © RhB, Andrea Badrutt
P. 210 © RhB Archive
P. 211 © Graubünden Tourism, Andrea Badrutt
P. 212-215 © Appenzeller Bahnen
P. 216 © SBB Historic
P. 217 © Muriel92/Shutterstock.com
P. 218-219 © RhB, Andrea Badrutt
P. 221 © Graubünden Tourism, Johannes Hüchelheim
P. 222 © SBB Historic
P. 223 © RhB, Andrea Badrutt
P. 225 © Jungfraubahnen
P. 227 © Rigi Bahnen AG, Brigitte Marty

INDEX

EXPLORE MORE OF SWITZERLAND WITH HELVETIQ:

Cartographica Helvetica

ISBN: 978-3-03869-115-0

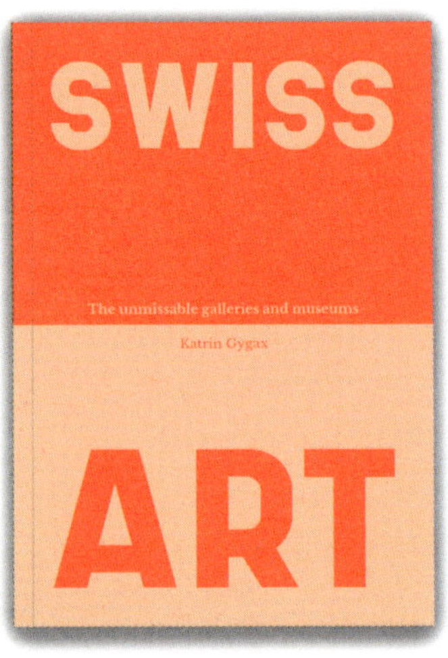

Swiss Art

ISBN: 978-3-03869-166-2

Helvetic Kitchen

ISBN: 978-3-03869-128-0

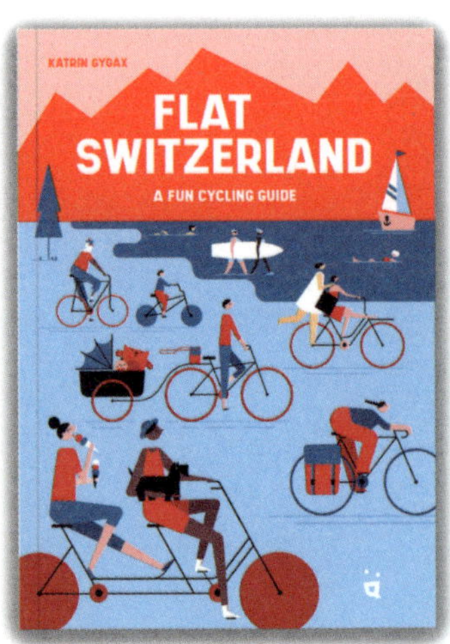

Flat Switzerland

ISBN: 978-3-907293-67-6